COASTAL WATERS
A Management Analysis

By

JOHN M. ARMSTRONG
Associate Professor of Civil Engineering
Director, Coastal Zone Laboratory
University of Michigan
Ann Arbor, Michigan

PETER C. RYNER
Director, Coastal Resources
Planning and Analysis
The Traverse Group, Inc.
Ann Arbor, Michigan

ANN ARBOR SCIENCE
PUBLISHERS INC
P.O. BOX 1425 • ANN ARBOR, MICH. 48106

Portions of research activities that contributed to this analysis
of coastal water management were supported by the Office of
Coastal Zone Management, NOAA, U.S. Department of Commerce. The views and findings in this book are solely those of
the authors and do not reflect any policy or recommendation of
the Government.

PREFACE

For the past several years there has been a growing interest and concern in the U.S. with the management of ocean and coastal resources. Since 1972 there has been considerable activity in the area of coastal resource management. Much of this work has been under the provisions of the Federal Coastal Zone Management Act of 1972. The individual coastal states have been developing comprehensive programs aimed at both protecting and developing coastal resources.

The objective of this book is to establish an overview of the factors that will be involved in the states' efforts to establish comprehensive management and planning programs for their coastal waters. Stress is placed on the spatial and temporal boundaries of coastal *waters*, rather than on the more frequently discussed coastal *lands*. This emphasis is deliberate in an attempt to establish a more balanced approach in future state coastal management efforts that have often placed primary emphasis on land and shore considerations.

Four major themes are presented: a description of various uses of coastal waters and the implications of those uses for comprehensive management; a description and analysis of existing bases of authority to manage coastal *waters*; a discussion of the Coastal Zone Management Act in terms of its utility for managing coastal waters; and a presentation of some concepts for coastal water management.

The intended audience for this book are planners, managers and researchers involved in the development of ocean and coastal resource management policies and programs.

CONTENTS

PART 1   INTRODUCTION

PART 2   AUTHORITY TO MANAGE COASTAL WATERS

PART 3   COASTAL WATER USES AND ACTIVITIES

PART 4   MANAGEMENT CONCEPTS

John M. Armstrong is Associate Professor at the University of
Michigan, Department of Civil Engineering. Dr. Armstrong received
his undergraduate and graduate degrees in engineering from the
University of Michigan. He has served as Director of the University
of Michigan Sea Grant Program and is presently Director of the
University of Michigan Coastal Zone Laboratory. He is a consultant
to governments and to industry in the areas of coastal resource
policy analysis and management program development, and has
published numerous technical papers and reports.

Peter C. Ryner is Director, Coastal Resources Planning and Analysis,
The Traverse Group, Inc., Ann Arbor, Michigan. He specializes in
shorelands planning and resource policy. Mr. Ryner received his
MS in resource planning and conservation from the University of
Michigan. His work in the field includes creation of workshops,
media presentations, public hearings and a number of technical
publications.

PART 1

INTRODUCTION

CHAPTER 1

INTRODUCTION

SCOPE

Use of the nation's coastal waters is increasing at a rapid pace. The acceleration of offshore oil development, proposals for deepwater ports, plans for floating power plants, and increased emphasis on fisheries management have all served to highlight the importance of coastal waters. Current and potential conflicts over use of coastal waters are also developing at a comparable rate.

The Coastal Zone Management Act was created to deal with the complex questions of allocation and protection of coastal resources. Many states have or are now developing management programs for coastal lands and for estuarine and nearshore waters. But in many instances, little emphasis has been placed on the water areas of the territorial sea and the adjacent ocean waters. The basic premise of this report is that most states have given considerable attention to shore and nearshore areas, but that in implementing approved Sec. 306 programs, the complexities and opportunities of the broader coastal territorial sea must be given more attention. An attempt is made here to introduce the concept of comprehensive coastal *water* planning and management as part of a more general coastal zone management system. Little consideration is given here to estuarine or coastal land planning or management, although they are at present of primary consideration to many coastal states. Rather, the offshore water issues are stressed in an effort to encourage

3

increased consideration of how these management issues can be incorporated within the framework of the Coastal Zone Management Act of 1972.

DEFINITIONS

The term coastal waters is defined in the Coastal Zone Management Act (CZMA) as:

1. In the Great Lakes area, waters within the territorial jurisdiction of the United States, consisting of the Great Lakes, their connecting waters, harbors, roadsteads, and estuary-type areas such as bays, shallows, and marshes.

2. In other areas, waters adjacent to the shorelines which contain a measurable quantity or percentage of sea water, including, but not limited to sounds, bays, lagoons, bayous, ponds, and estuaries. [Sec. 304(b)]

Section 304 (h) defines water use as including:

Activities which are conducted in or on the water; but does not mean or include the establishment of any water quality standard or criteria or the regulation of the discharge or runoff of water pollutants except the standards, criteria, or regulations which are incorporated in any program as required by the provisions of Section 307 (f).

However, for the purposes of this book, "coastal waters" and "coastal water use" will be defined both more generally and more narrowly. Focus will be on the human use of the territorial sea, including the Great Lakes, and upon human activities taking place in the oceans beyond, to the degree that they may affect coastal waters. A first definition used in this report, is:

"Coastal waters" will include the submerged lands, the water column, the surface waters, and to some degree, the air above the territorial waters of the United States. Except in the Gulf of Mexico, this will be limited to a three-mile-wide band of water.

THE CONCEPT OF COMPREHENSIVE
COASTAL WATER USE MANAGEMENT

As used in this book, comprehensive coastal water use planning and management refers to the concept of integrating a

growing number of human activities within a water activity
arena that has certain natural limitations and inherent values
that must be recognized and protected. There are three primary goals, each of which is similar to those of the more
general field of coastal zone management.

Conflict Resolution

With increased use of the submerged lands, water column
and surface waters of the coastal zone, more attention must be
given to designing activity patterns to minimize disruptions or
conflicts among users. For coastal states, this may include a
need to resolve conflicts between local, state or federal governments; to consider domestic versus international interests in the
use of coastal waters; to improve coordination between state
and federal programs; and to sort out physically the growing
number of uses of submerged lands, coastal waters and the air
above. The issues are complex as are emerging conflicts between coastal and ocean water, land and water, and air and
water uses.

However, conflict resolution is not the same as comprehensive
resource planning and management, although in some instances
conflict resolution has been made the sole objective of a management effort. It is suggested that while conflict resolution is
an essential and difficult part of coastal water planning and
management, it also is more of a means to a more comprehensive objective, rather than the primary reason for coastal
management.

Increased Coastal Water Use

As reflected in the language of the Coastal Zone Management
Act and other legislation, such as the Outer Continental Shelf
Lands Act, there is a national interest in expanding the use of
coastal waters, and of the oceans beyond. Any increased use is
likely to generate further conflicts and intensify pressures upon
the natural systems of the coastal zone. However, it is not
clear that we have yet developed the capacity to sustain present
levels and types of use while also sustaining a viable natural
ocean system. In addition, the United States has an expanding

population with a need for recreation, food, transportation, national defense and employment. Our economic system tends to treat the coastal waters as potential resources, to be extracted and processed for human benefit. Consequently, under the explicit directions of Congress, to the degree that expanded use can be achieved without disrupting necessary current patterns of use or destroying the marine environment, such expansion must be attempted. This suggests the need for positive action to discover methods for accommodating activities rather than simply reacting to potential adverse impacts once a project is proposed.

Protection and Enhancement of the Marine Environment

Historically, coastal waters have been viewed as an aquatic setting for human activities and as a source of potential resources for human use. Also, coastal waters have historically been treated as a vast dumping ground into which virtually every type of human waste, including toxic and explosive substances, have been deposited. Fish have been harvested as if they existed in infinite numbers. The marine system is fragile, finite and of immense importance not only to adjacent communities but also for global air quality, food supplies, weather and climatic patterns.

Species of plants, mammals, birds and fish have been diminished or eliminated. Critical breeding grounds, nursery areas and food webs have been damaged, contaminated or lost. Frequently, any additional human use of coastal waters places increased pressures upon the marine environment. The system has limits. If the coastal waters are to continue to support finfish and shellfish, and provide recreational opportunities, and if their capacity to support a wide variety of activities is to be protected, then human activities must be limited, modified and in some instances prohibited, to fit within the constraints of the finite capacities of natural systems. If these capacities are more precisely understood, then expanded use is more likely. And if the natural system is maintained at a high quality level, the maximum number of human uses can occur. The consequences of not treating natural capacities as constraints to human use of coastal waters are not clear. But they may include adverse shifts in weather and climate patterns, loss of food supplies and of food production capability, deterioration of adjacent land values, loss of major recreational opportunities, and a considerable diminution of the economic potential of these resources.

In focusing on planning and management of the coastal waters, there is a danger of suggesting an artificial separation of land, air and water planning, which would violate the principal integrative concepts of the Coastal Zone Management Act. Clearly, coastal water use planning and management must be integrated within a comprehensive coastal zone management program. However, as this book attempts to illustrate, the present network of public laws and human activities associated with the coastal waters of the United States is very complex, not clearly defined, and will require considerable attention if state coordination of coastal uses is to be successful.

THE IMPORTANCE OF COASTAL WATERS

There are several reasons why coastal states might benefit from greater consideration of coastal water use management:

Growth of Offshore Activities

The Commission on Marine Science Engineering and Resources provided a good description of the expanding use of coastal and ocean resources in its report, *Our Nation and the Sea.* As the Commission stressed (p. 52), "problems of multiple uses of the coastal zone are moving seaward." Accelerated OCS lease sales, growing interest in storage of wastes in subsurface areas, the possibility of offshore geothermal energy sources, new national interest in fisheries management, increased liquefied natural gas shipments, floating power plants, deepwater ports and many other activities indicate that utilization of coastal waters and the ocean beyond will expand with or without a comprehensive management system. If the resource base is to be protected from unwise use, if conflicts are to minimized, and if priority uses are to be accommodated, a planning and management system will be a necessity.

Impacts of Water Use upon Land Use

In many instances, decisions regarding OCS or coastal water activities may determine what the coastal zone is or can be. As use of coastal and ocean waters intensifies, so will the requests for various types of shore access. This includes not only a new demand for harbor and port facilities, marinas, boat ramps, parking lots and beaches, but also suggests an unprecedented demand for heliports, tank farms, landfall sites for pipelines, LNG storage facilities, fish processing plants, military bases and transportation systems. Growth and change within coastal communities may seem "inevitable" and beyond public control unless the water-based pressures generating such growth and change are identified and managed.

Requirements of the Coastal Zone Management Act

The Act requires that approved coastal management programs be able to regulate activities that may have a direct or significant impact upon coastal waters. Priorities for coastal land and water uses are to be identified along with permissible uses. Thus, it is assumed that coastal states will at some point have a planning and management logic for determining which activities should be permitted, which should be prohibited, and which given priority access to the coastal waters of the state. Unless a comprehensive approach to coastal water activities and their relationship to ocean and shore issues is undertaken, it may be increasingly difficult to have any basis for determining priorities, or for knowing what should and should not occur within the coastal zone.

Coastal Waters as a Unique, High Value State Resource

Coastal states and their local communities are well aware of the economic, social, environmental and aesthetic values derived from their coastal waters. The Coastal Zone Management Act provides a jurisdictional framework and financial assistance to develop a long-range comprehensive planning and management system for this resource. Given the complexity and expense of such an undertaking, most states would not attempt anything approaching a comprehensive planning and management effort for their coastal waters without the assistance of the Act. It is an unusual opportunity at a particularly important time in the history of coastal and ocean development. Hopefully this discussion will assist states and others in taking full advantage of it.

"Consistency" Review of Federal Activities

Under Section 307 of the Coastal Zone Management Act of 1972, coastal states with an approved management program can, to some degree, protect the integrity of their program through consistency review of activities sponsored or approved by federal agencies—a key feature of the Coastal Zone Management Act; and under the current ambiguous distribution of management authority over coastal waters, it is also a deciding factor in the degree of state ability to manage coastal water activities. Just what "consistency" means is something that will evolve over time; final rules and regulations for Section 307 have not yet been formulated. However, there is an initial indication that some federal agencies may provide coastal states with information for consistency review on a very controlled basis, limited to the specific items articulated within the state's approved coastal zone management plan (CZMP). Even if this does not occur, it seems clearly advantageous for coastal states to include the most detailed and comprehensive statement possible of their goals, priorities and concerns. Because of concern about land and nearshore problems, some states may have overlooked the long-range implications of not developing a detailed program for the rest of the territorial sea. It is in deepwater areas where the federal interest is more traditional, the distribution of authority most unclear, and the likelihood for dispute over the right of a state to review or object to a federal action the strongest.

SPECIAL PROBLEMS OF COASTAL WATER USE PLANNING AND MANAGEMENT

Special Sensitivities of Coastal Waters

As a result of their physical and chemical properties, coastal waters can transmit impacts rapidly for great distances. Coastal waters also contain a series of interconnected biological systems often quite sensitive to environmental variation, therefore any change induced by human use has a potential for damage. For the most part, coastal waters have proven to be remarkably resilient to human modifications. But complex webs of current patterns, thermal regimes, nutrient cycles and species interactions are not immune to impact. Management programs should recognize that coastal waters are biologically and chemically far more reactive than coastal lands.

Size of the System to be Managed

It can be both technically difficult and expensive to inventory, monitor and regulate use of coastal lands. However, the submerged lands, water column and surface waters of the territorial sea represent an entirely new level of planning and management challenge, as the size and complexity of coastal waters are usually several times larger than the land elements of a coastal zone. Just knowing what is happening can be a major challenge. Complex computer control systems for surface vessel traffic may soon be established in major port areas by the U.S. Coast Guard. The Navy already has radar/communications/computer/administrative networks of great complexity and sophistication to manage its coastal and ocean operations. Most states will find it useful, if not necessary, to obtain assistance from federal agencies, universities and private industry if they are to collect and utilize the amount and type of information which comprehensive coastal waters management may eventually require. In addition, enforcement of coastal water management policies and regulations over the broad expanse of submerged lands and water may require a new type of law enforcement organization and expenditure, for both local and state government.

Established Patterns of Use

Complex patterns of coastal water use already exist as a result of historic development, implied dedication, crown gifts, state leases or prior management decisions. The coastal waters are not "empty space" but, in fact, a crowded mixture of interacting natural systems and human claims to present or future patterns of use.

Many coastal water areas are informally allocated for fishing activities, based upon the port from which fishing occurs. These aquatic territories have often been quite strictly enforced, by fishermen, and new public comprehensive management systems must acknowledge the existence of such patterns of use and somehow deal with them. Similarly, the submerged lands often contain polluted sediment, canisters of hazardous materials, or large amounts of solid waste resulting from previous coastal water activities. Present and past water uses have established prior claims that require management consideration in any new allocation. In addition they have often modified the coastal environment in ways that may represent major management problems or opportunities.

Special Legal Considerations

In sharp contrast with coastal lands, there is very little private ownership of coastal waters, especially beyond the nearshore or littoral area. However, there are leases, grants, licenses and riparian patterns of use which, if not always having the full force of proprietary rights, can nonetheless exert an influence over who can do what in coastal waters. There is an extensive body of special maritime law that applies to most coastal water areas and activities. This adds an altogether new complexity as well as a predetermined set of decision rules to coastal water management that will not be found on land (see also Chapter Two). Coastal managers must be aware of this special law if they hope to successfully implement a coastal water management program.

There are several international treaties, accords and agreements which either now influence or may in the future affect the control or use of coastal waters. While state ownership of the submerged lands beneath coastal waters may be widely recognized, the ability of the coastal state to control surface use of coastal waters is constrained by federal and international concepts of navigational servitude. The principle of allowing innocent passage of foreign ships within territorial waters is but one of these concepts. Pending revisions of international maritime law may add further complications that state coastal programs must consider.

Special Significance of Management Decisions

It is difficult to fully appreciate the importance of coastal waters and the management decisions made for them. To some extent, coastal *land* use decisions made at the community or state level will primarily affect local and state interests, although there are obvious and important exceptions to this observation. On the other hand, coastal *water* decisions are almost always connected economically, militarily, biologically and chemically to the waters of adjacent states and to the federal and international waters and submerged lands beyond. Coastal waters are the interface between local and international concerns; state and federal jurisdiction, and domestic and international law.

1. World as well as regional and local climate and weather systems are influenced by coastal and ocean waters. Tides, currents, thermal regimes and the carbon dioxide balance of the atmosphere are involved. Coastal and ocean production of oxygen is of global significance, and it takes place at the sensitive and easily polluted water/air interface. Thermal modification of coastal waters, either deliberately or as a secondary consequence of use, may have major impact far beyond the limits of states' coastal waters.

2. Coastal and adjacent ocean waters serve as a vital national and international transportation medium, the disruption of which could have serious consequences.

3. Coastal waters are a major national and international source of food, and the importance of this may well increase.

4. Coastal waters may increasingly serve as a direct source of energy (waves, tides, temperature gradients). Hydrocarbons and possibly significant amounts of methane or geothermal energy are or may be contained beneath coastal waters. Energy-related storage, production, and transportation systems use and often are dependent upon a coastal water location.

5. Coastal waters are a vital part of national defense, and coastal water use management decisions could have major national security implications.

The Federal Presence

This may be the single most complex and important part of coastal water use management for state program managers. One of the most prominent characteristics of coastal waters is the degree to which they are associated with federal programs, authorities and agencies. These federal interests in some instances represent an exclusive right over some aspect of coastal water use. In *all* instances, careful consideration should be given to what the national interest might be in a coastal water use decision, and which federal agencies or authorities might be involved.

The Federal Water Pollution Control Act (FWPCA) amendments of 1972 represent one good example of this. This legislation established as national policy the elimination of pollution discharge into coastal (and other) waters by 1985. This could produce an immense impact upon what coastal water uses can or should occur, where they should be located, and how they should be designed and undertaken. The FWPCA also deals with aquaculture, dredge spoil disposal, vessel discharge and oil spills. This and other federal legislation establish a network of standards, processes and authorities that is as important a part of coastal water use planning and management as the complex interconnected biogeochemical and energy systems of the marine environment.

CONCLUSIONS

It has been suggested that comprehensive coastal water management is too complex; that the task is too great; or that it is unrealistic to expect a state to attempt, much less implement, so difficult, large and expensive a program.

At present, it is probably true that no state could create and implement a total coastal water use management system. It is not yet clear that there is a need for such a system, but use is increasing. Pressures upon the natural capabilities of the marine environment are having visible effect, and the Coastal Zone Management Act recognizes that someone must take a long-range look at this essential national resource, and assume responsibility for its continued vitality and utility.

The actual cost, in terms of time, energy, money, people and equipment, to effect such planning and management may be far beyond what has been presently estimated by Congress, as reflected in the provisions and funding of the Coastal Zone Management Act. Expanded use will require more management and more coordination between local, state and federal interests. Such coordination and management costs money, and the amount will increase as does our need to use and protect these resources.

While this is a major problem that will require further consideration, states should realize the degree to which the present web of federal agencies and laws represent a coastal water management *resource*. It would be naive to suggest that every federal agency is presently willing or able to provide all the assistance a state may seek. The management of state resources is primarily a state responsibility and will undoubtedly remain so as long as states wish to retain management control. However, federal use of coastal and ocean resources do impart costs upon state and local government. The Coastal Energy Impact Program (CEIP) of the Coastal Zone Management Act is one attempt to deal with this problem.

More importantly, each federal agency having an interest in or responsibility for coastal water use also has information and experience. The Coast Guard has techniques, equipment, experience and a mandate to enforce coastal regulations. The Environmental Protection Agency (EPA) conducts or sponsors extensive research on the impact of various activities and substances on coastal waters. Other agencies have maps, computer programs, publications, photographs and related forms of information and equipment. Some of this will not be available to states. Others will need updating or modification, while some will just not be applicable. However, a large portion of the available resources will benefit coastal planning and management. Cooperative efforts in areas of mutual concern are not only possible, but crucial.

The importance of establishing a comprehensive coastal water management program as part of a state's total coastal zone management program is far greater than many states may have yet perceived. The difficulties in achieving a comprehensive coastal water use management capability are, to say the least, considerable. But the Coastal Zone Management Act provides the states with several tools. It provides national recognition of the states as the appropriate management coordinator for federal cooperation and assistance. It recognizes the right of states to review any federal activity that will impact the coastal waters, and to consider how and if those activities might affect the coastal water use management plan.

Comprehensive coastal water use management, as well as a national ocean policy, are things of the future . . . but of the near future. No state has yet attempted a comprehensive coastal water management program. Yet for many river basins, as well as for bays, sounds and nearshore waters, such a comprehensive approach has started, and some would say has been achieved. Every coastal state has some coastal water use regulations, as with submerged lands leasing or fisheries management. These can be expanded, modified and integrated into more comprehensive management systems as the need arises. New federal laws, if they are written to directly acknowledge the approved state coastal management program, could specify a coordinated state/federal effort when new program inventories are made or new standards established.

As should be clear from reading this material, changes in laws and funding may be necessary. New ideas and new information will be needed. However, even now a creative use of the Coastal Zone Management Act, along with the other local, state and federal programs, should allow the establishment of a basic integrated management program that can protect, enhance and allocate the submerged lands, water column and surface waters of the coastal zone, as part of an overall state resource management effort. It is hoped that this initial consideration of that concept will further such attempts.

PART 2

AUTHORITY TO MANAGE COASTAL WATERS

CHAPTER 2

STATE AUTHORITY TO MANAGE COASTAL WATERS

The Coastal Zone Management Act of 1972 provides a mechanism for the establishment of state programs to protect and develop coastal waters. However, it is not always clear what actual powers of management or control the various coastal states have over specific coastal water activities and resources. As the planning and management of these resources becomes a matter of increasing concern, the issue of jurisdiction will become a crucial factor.

This chapter attempts to provide the state coastal manager with some initial guidance to present legislative and judicial determinations of state powers to control coastal water use. This is not a technical legal guide, but a management-oriented discussion of basic state and federal sources of authority. The remainder of Part Two continues the discussion or jurisdiction into specific activities, and should be read in conjunction with this chapter.

The CZMA, in Section 302 (h), states that the key to more effective protection and use of the land and water resources of the coastal zone is:

> . . . to encourage the states to exercise *their full authority* over the lands and waters in the coastal zone . . . . (emphasis added)

Since this "full authority" is not delineated in the Act, it must be surmised from other legislation as well as court decisions. The political, legislative and judicial history of national coastal water policy indicates that the distribution of authority is fluid and evolving.

However, there are some relatively explicit allocations of authority which provide tentative guidance for state program implementation. The first section of this chapter traces the judicial and legislative history of coastal management leading up to the passage of the Submerged Lands Act and Outer Continental Shelf Lands Act. The second section discusses certain constitutional and congressional provisions that limit or further define the nature of state authority over coastal waters. Chapter Three describes specific acts and federal agencies that relate to coastal water use management.

HISTORY OF DEVELOPMENT OF STATE AND FEDERAL AUTHORITY

As technology, national policy and economic factors stimulated greater interest in the use of the resources of the nation's territorial seas and submerged lands, there emerged a growing and continuing dispute over what powers the coastal states should or do have to regulate or control these resources and their use.

Until the 1920s there were few major disagreements over whether states could regulate coastal waters. In part this followed from a limited technical and economic ability to utilize coastal water resources, especially oil and gas deposits in submerged lands. There also appears to have been a general acceptance on the part of both federal and state government that states had a basic authority to regulate coastal water resources.[1]

But in the late 1920s, offshore extraction of oil and gas became feasible, and by the mid-1930s there was a growing concern by both state and federal authority about who might have jurisdiction over the submerged lands.[2] Of significance is that much of the dispute that followed, and much of the key legislation was related to submerged lands rather than surface waters or the water column. The control of oil and gas deposits and of the billions of dollars of revenue involved in such control has been the focus of many of the disputes over state versus federal rights, and was a primary topic of several major U.S. Supreme Court decisions to be discussed in following sections. This historic emphasis upon oil and gas production helps explain some of the provisions of legislation such as the Outer Continental Shelf Lands Act and the Submerged Lands Act, and also suggests that authority over surface waters and the water column may require further clarification.

By the mid-1940s the federal government was making a strong claim to paramount control over all coastal resources, rejecting *any* state claim to ownership or jurisdiction. This was reflected in the Truman Proclamation of September 28, 1945, which claimed exclusive U.S. jurisdiction over the natural resources of the continental shelf, and in a series of federal challenges to state control of submerged lands in the U.S. Supreme Court.

In three landmark decisions (*U.S. v. California, 1947,* 332 U.S. 19; *U.S. v. Texas, 1950,* 339 U.S. 707; *U.S. v. Louisiana, 1950,* 339 U.S. 699), the U. S. Supreme Court held that the federal government, rather than the states, had paramount rights in the submerged lands and natural resources of the territorial seas of the United States.

> The United States of America is now, and has been at all times pertinent hereto, possessed of paramount rights in, and full dominion and power over, the lands, minerals, and other things underlying the Pacific Ocean lying seaward of the ordinary low-water mark on the coast of California, and outside of the inland waters, extending seaward three nautical miles . . . . *The state of California has no title thereto or property interest therein.*[3] (emphasis added)

Several coastal states saw this as a denial of their basic constitutional rights, a "power-grab" by the federal government. Louisiana, Texas and California were primarily concerned about control over oil revenues. But several other coastal states saw nonoil-related issues involved in this declaration of total federal jurisdiction. Robert Moses of New York State expressed concern over the future control of Jones Beach and other projects that had been claimed from the sea. New England fishing interests saw this as a threat to their industry, and Great Lakes representatives joined in a strong expression of concern over states' rights.[4]

The question of coastal jurisdiction became a major national political issue. It was the topic of 15 congressional hearings, was in part responsible for the resignation of Harold Ickes as Secretary of Interior, and was a major topic of debate in the 1952 presidential campaign, during which Dwight Eisenhower promised to support state control of submerged lands.

In 1953, newly elected President Eisenhower signed into law the Submerged Lands Act of 1953 and the Outer Continental Shelf Act of 1953. As discussed in more detail below, these acts gave primary control over the submerged lands of coastal waters to the states, and to submerged lands beyond the territorial sea to the federal government.

But the debate over jurisdiction was not silenced by the passage of these laws. In the late 1960s, a continued disagreement between several coastal states and the federal government led to another major Supreme Court case which was finally decided in favor of the federal government in 1974.

The *United States v. Maine* case was precipitated by a lease of submerged lands for oil and gas development by the state of Maine. The federal government sought to get a final definite articulation by the Supreme Court of who had jurisdiction over the seabed and natural resources beyond the territorial or coastal sea. It raised the issue not only against Maine, but also against New Hampshire, Massachusetts, Rhode Island, New Jersey, Delaware, Maryland, Virginia, North Carolina, South Carolina, Georgia and Florida. In a report prepared by a court-appointed Special Master,[5] the following was determined:

1. The Truman Proclamation of 1945 for the first time claimed for the United States jurisdiction and control over the natural resources of the subsoil and seabed of the continental shelf beyond the three-mile limit of the territorial sea off the coasts of the United States. The Proclamation initiated a new rule of international law in this regard.

2. This claim was validly made by and on behalf of the United States under its powers of external sovereignty and did not insure to the individual benefit of any of the Atlantic coastal states.

3. By the Submerged Lands Act of May 22, 1953, 67 Stat. 29, the United States confirmed to and vested in the defendant states the seabed and the resources of the territorial sea within three geographical miles of their respective coastlines (Florida and Texas granted jurisdiction out to three marine leagues, based on historic boundaries).

4. Under the Truman Proclamation, the Outer Continental
   Shelf Lands Act of 1953, and the Convention on the Continental Shelf of 1964, the United States has the right, *as
   against* the defendant states, to the resources of the seabed
   and subsoil of the continental shelf beyond the three-mile
   limit of territorial sea off the Atlantic coast.

While some coastal states have indicated a strong disagreement
with both this finding and the earlier findings of the late
1940s and early 1950s, it presently can be taken as the law of
the land that state jurisdiction over ocean resources is restricted
to the territorial sea of the coastal zone.

In future coastal water use disputes, the ability or lack of it
to intercede in decisions related to coastal water use beyond
the present territorial boundaries may determine the effectiveness of a state management program.

The scope of the Coastal Zone Management Act is limited
specifically "seaward to the outer limit of the United States
territorial sea."[6]   The federal government recently declared partial jurisdiction over ocean resources out to a distance of 200
miles for the purpose of fishery management. If a full extension of the territorial boundary should occur, the question may
arise as to whether that also extends the current limit of the
Coastal Zone Management Act.

However, the Office of Coastal Zone Management has made
an explicit ruling over the scope of the Act. In an OCZM
Threshold Paper related to boundaries, waters beyond the present three-mile (or three leagues in the Gulf of Mexico) territorial
limit must *not* be included in an approved state coastal management program.

Waters beyond the three-mile territorial sea.

Irrespective of any extended seaward jurisdiction which may be
enacted by law or agreed to under international convention,
states may not include waters beyond the territorial sea, in the
absence of specific legislation.[7]   (emphasis added)

Submerged Lands Act of 1953[8]

The basic federal recognition and specification of state authority to regulate coastal water use is contained in the Submerged
Lands Act. This allocation of jurisdictional authority emerged
from a 30-year federal/state conflict described earlier in this book.

The stated purpose of this Act is:

> To confirm and establish the titles of the states to *lands
> beneath navigable waters* within state boundaries and to
> *the natural resources within such lands and waters,* to pro-
> vide for the use and control of said lands and resources,
> and to confirm the jurisdiction and control of the United
> States over the natural resources of the seabed of the con-
> tinental shelf seaward of state boundaries. (emphasis added)

The Act indicates a broad definition of natural resources, and on its face, would seem to include virtually all living and nonliving resources on or beneath the ocean floor or within the water column.

> Section 2 (e). The term "natural resources" includes with-
> out limiting the generality thereof, oil, gas, and all other
> minerals, and fish, shrimp, oysters, clams, crabs, lobsters,
> sponges, kelp, and other marine animal and plant life, but
> does not include water power, or the use of water for the
> production of power.

The significance of the last provision, which clearly reserves the use of waters for power production to the federal government, may increase in the near future. Both France and England are giving serious consideration to either tidal power production or to the use of wave energy for the production of electricity. Similar proposals have been made in the United States. While the Coastal Zone Management Act indicates a congressional in- tention to have the coastal states be the prime coastal water managers, this provision of the Submerged Lands Act may affect their ability to regulate water-based power production projects.

SLA Limitations upon State Authority

The Submerged Lands Act specifically excludes several areas of authority from state control.

1. Section 3 (d): "Nothing in this Act shall affect the use,
   development, improvement, or control by or under the constitutional authority of the United States of said lands and
   waters for the purposes of *navigation* or *flood control* or
   the *production of power* . . . ." (emphasis added)

2. Section 6 (a): "The United States retains all its *navigational
   servitude* and rights in and powers of said lands and navigable

waters for the constitutional purposes of *commerce, navigation, national defense and international affairs* . . . ."
(emphasis added)

3. Section 6 (b): "In time of war or when necessary for national defense, and the Congress or the President shall so prescribe, the United States shall have the right of first refusal to purchase at the prevailing market price, all or any portion of the said natural resources, or *to acquire and use any portion of said lands* by proceeding in accordance with due process of law and paying just compensation therefore."
(emphasis added)

The extent to which the above exclusions diminish the power of the states to manage coastal water activities is not clear. In each instance it is a question of the facts of the case, of state and federal assertions, of political forces, and of judicial interpretation. In the next section, several federal constitutionally derived powers will be discussed to indicate that words such as commerce, navigation, national defense or international affairs can relate to virtually every aspect of coastal water management.

AUTHORITIES AS ALLOCATED IN THE U.S. CONSTITUTION

Review of Basic State Powers

The state has two basic sources of power over coastal waters. One derives from ownership (to the degree that the Submerged Lands Act or other laws acknowledge state ownership) and secondly, as sovereign protector of the health, safety and welfare of the citizens of the state. In principle, these police powers are reserved by the states unless specifically granted to the federal government (see tenth amendment of Constitution).

Three basic rules influence the degree to which a state may be able to regulate coastal waters through its police powers. The Supreme Court has held that:

1. any state regulation must have a legitimate public purpose: that it is necessary to protect the health, safety, or general welfare of its citizens;

2. given a legitimate public purpose, the specific regulation in question must be directly related to that purpose; and

3. if the regulation results in a "taking" of property, but is otherwise necessary and reasonable, there must be just compensation to the property owner.

In general it is held that the state must be reasonable and must not be arbitrary or capricious. This has translated in recent years into a need for a formal process of decision-making, public input and provision for appeal of a regulation. But there are several areas in which the state has been found by the Supreme Court to be either totally excluded from or to have definite limitations upon its use of police powers.

It appears that the intent of Congress in formulating the Coastal Zone Management Act was not to alter the existent distribution of coastal jurisdiction between federal and state sources. In Section 307 (e), an important and explicit statement regarding this issue is made:

> Section 307 (e). Nothing in this title shall be construed (1) to diminish either federal or state jurisdiction, responsibility, or rights in the field of planning, development, or control of water resources, submerged lands, or navigable waters . . ."

The Act is even more explicit in the following subsection, where it is stated that:

> Section 307 (e). (Nothing in this title shall be construed) (2) as superseding, modifiying, or repealing existing laws applicable to the various federal agencies . . . .

The Submerged Lands Act of 1953 and the Outer Continental Shelf Lands Act of 1953 appear to provide a clear delineation of authority over coastal submerged lands with state control specified out to the three-mile boundary (or three leagues in Gulf Coast) and federal control beyond. However, even that division is not absolute. When considering the living resources within the water column or nonextractive uses of surface or subsurface waters, there tends to be a strong judicial and legislative recognition of federal interest, if not paramount control, even within the territorial sea. While Congress has made it clear that the Coastal Zone Management Act of 1972 is intended to allow the states to serve as primary managers of coastal waters, Congress has also made clear that the Act does not diminish existent federal power or authority. Much of the basis for that federal authority is either implicit or explicit in the Constitution.

The Supremacy Clause (Article VI, Clause 2)

A basic articulation of federal authority over state interests lies in this clause, which declares:

> This Constitution, and the laws of the United States which shall be made in pursuance thereof; and all treaties made, or which shall be made, under the authority of the United States, shall be the supreme law of the land; and the judges in every state shall be bound thereby; anything in the Constitution or laws of any state to the contrary not withstanding.

Limitations upon state power are contained both within the Constitution and, as the supremacy clause states, within federal statue or treaty.

The Commerce Clause (Article I, Section 8, Clause 3)

The Commerce Clause of the Constitution provides a major source of federal authority in coastal waters, and is also perhaps the single most important limitation that the Constitution places upon state power.[9] The language within the Constitution is brief, indicating only that Congress has power to "regulate commerce with foreign nations and among the several states . . . ." But as Power observes:[10] "Over the years the Supreme Court has given this simple language such an expansive interpretation that today Congress has substantially unfettered control over the nation's waterways."

In 1824 the U.S. Supreme Court held, in *Gibbons v. Ogden*, that commerce includes transportation which includes navigation. Since then, the term navigable waters has been extended in concept by the courts to allow the federal government jurisdiction over nonnavigable tributaries of a navigable water (*U.S. v. Ashland Oil and Transportation Company*).[11]

But the commerce clause goes far beyond control of navigation, and it is not limited to commerce. As decided in *United States v. Appalachian Power Company*:

> It cannot properly be said that the constitutional power of the
> United States over its waters is limited to control for navigation . . . .
> That authority is as broad as the needs of commerce . . . . Flood
> protection, watershed development, recovery of the costs of im-
> provements through utilization of power are likewise parts of
> commerce control.[12]

The Supreme Court has also ruled that the commerce clause
extends beyond interstate commerce to include those actions
within a state that might affect interstate commerce:

> The commerce power is not confined in its exercise to the
> regulation of commerce among the states . . . (i)t extends to
> those activities intrastate which so affect interstate commerce
> . . . to make regulation of them appropriate . . . no form of
> state activity can constitutionally thwart the power granted by
> the commerce clause to Congress.[13]

Treaties or Alliances (Article I, Section 10, Clause I)

The Constitution forbids any state to enter into any "Treaty,
Alliance, or Confederation . . ." with any foreign power. As
Wroth observes,[14] this prohibition is of considerable importance.
It precludes a coastal state from entering into an independent
treaty with an adjacent foreign nation in regard to such matters
as regulation of fisheries or pollution control. Thus a state
must defer to the federal government in matters relating to
foreign governments, as well as to matters falling within the
broad category of commerce.

Article II, Section 2 of the Constitution specifically reserves
for the federal government the right to make treaties. There
have been some disputes over the extent of this power, with
states arguing that the federal government has used this clause
to infringe upon powers reserved to the states under the tenth
amendment.[15]

With both explicit legislative authority and extensive jurisdiction through court interpretation of the commerce clause, there
may be little federal interest in using the treaties provision in
jurisdictional disputes with coastal states. Yet international
accords may form a substantive part of national marine policy,
and this remains an important federal power.

Power over Foreign Affairs

In *Perez v. Brownell*[16] the Supreme Court found that even though there is no specific grant to the federal government of full power over foreign affairs in the Constitution, that such powers are, of necessity, an inherent tool of Congress. This in part derives from the treaty powers cited above.

The implications of this inherent power may be significant in coastal water planning and management. As an example, the 1947 Supreme Court decision in *United States v. California,* where the court ruled that the states had *no* authority over coastal waters, was based primarily upon the concept of a necessary federal control over coastal waters as part of its power over foreign affairs.

The Submerged Lands Act and the Coastal Zone Management Act provide considerable authority to the states, especially over submerged lands within the territorial sea. However, if regulating surface or water column activities affect foreign nationals or foreign governments, this implied or inherent federal authority may come into effect.

Admiralty Jurisdiction and Maritime Law (Article III, Section 2)

Through Article III, Section 2, federal courts are given power over all cases of admiralty and maritime jurisdiction. Congress used this constitutional power to establish the Judiciary Act of 1789 which further articulates the distribution of state and federal power over maritime law issues:

> . . . The district courts . . . shall also have exclusive original cognizance of all civil cases of admiralty and maritime jurisdiction . . . . [17]

This clause and the maritime law associated with it has two principal effects upon state efforts at managing coastal water activities: (a) It may determine in which courts a dispute will be settled, and (b) it may determine under what principles of law the courts are to resolve a particular issue.

To emphasize the potential significance of this clause, it is important to recognize that *while the state is not precluded from establishing coastal water regulations, they must be compatible with an extensive body of existent substantive law. In some instances legal disputes will, as a matter of law, be determined in federal district courts rather than in the common-law courts of the states.*

As with any matter of law, it is both difficult and potentially misleading to make general statements about the impact of admiralty jurisdiction and maritime law upon state coastal water management efforts. Each state manager is urged to consult directly with legal counsel when considering the establishment of coastal water regulations. With this caution in mind, some basic concepts are presented, based upon the discussion of Wroth:[18]

> Admiralty jurisdiction extends to all navigable waters, including inland waters capable of being navigated by vessels engaged in interstate or foreign commerce, even though such waters are wholly within a state. Thus all coastal states, including those of the Great Lakes region, would be affected.

> Through the Judiciary Act of 1789, Congress provided that suitors have the right to a common-law remedy, rather than through the admiralty courts, "where the common law is competent to give it . . . ."[17] Thus whether a case is to be heard in a United States District Court or in a state court is in some instances a matter of choice for the plaintiff, although there are several instances when as a matter of law, such cases must be heard in federal district court rather than state court.

> Of great importance is that federal maritime law principles may govern a case even if it is brought in state court. Maritime law derives in part from historic English admiralty law and in part from court decisions and acts of Congress. It is a substantive body of law with specific principles that may differ significantly from the law of a coastal state, and yet its principles may determine the decision of a case.

An Example

For those not familiar with admiralty jurisdiction and maritime law, a case cited by Wroth may help explain why the state coastal zone manager may wish to give detailed consideration to this body of law in developing and administering a coastal water use management effort.

In *Kossick v. United Fruit Company*,[19] the issue was raised as to whether New York State law or maritime law would determine the outcome of a dispute. The case involved an oral promise made by a shipowner to an injured seaman regarding possible compensation for his injuries. The Supreme Court held that because the case involved a seaman, and for associated reasons, that maritime law was involved. Of importance to state coastal managers is that the New York State law was bypassed, and the case was instead decided by principles of maritime law. Those principles include an ancient rule that oral promises constitute a firm and binding maritime contract, and it was on that basis that the case was decided. It will be of importance to consider maritime law and admiralty jurisdiction when dealing with the enforcement of coastal water management provisions. *Askew v. American Waterways* (see Chapter 10), focuses upon the extent to which admiralty law should affect a state management program. It is an important case for coastal water management, and is recommended for review.

Doctrine of Preemption

As management programs for coastal waters become more comprehensive, disputes may arise as to whether some new state regulation is preempted by federal authority (see Chapter 4). The preemption doctrine that has evolved through decisions of the Supreme Court holds that in instances where "compliance with both federal and state regulations is a physical impossibility" federal law will preempt state regulation (*Florida Lime and Avocado Growers, Inc. v. Paul*).[20] A factor that makes it especially difficult to clearly determine when preemption exists is that there need not be a clear conflict between state and federal laws. Preemption may also exist if the court determines that Congress intended to close an area from state authority.

The Coastal Zone Management Act, in Section 302 (h), indicates a strong congressional intent to have the states serve as lead authorities in establishing comprehensive coastal zone management programs. However, there are several explicit and implicit preemptions:

1. Section 307(e) has already been cited as an explicit declaration by Congress that the Coastal Zone Management Act will in no manner diminish present federal authority.

2. Section 307(f) declares that the Federal Water Pollution Control Act and the Clean Air Act requirements *shall be* the water pollution control and air pollution control requirements of state coastal management programs.

3. Section 307(g) indicates that if a national land use program is ever established it may have supremacy over shorelands plans of the states, and *will* require concurrence of the federal administrator of any national land use program with any state land elements in its coastal program.

In most instances, the question of how much control a coastal state can impose over coastal water activities will require a careful balancing of factors. The commerce clause, the supremacy clause, the doctrine of preemption, and the admiralty clause serve as major checks upon state authority in coastal waters, notwithstanding the provisions of the Submerged Lands Act, the Outer Continental Shelf Lands Act, or other legislation.

However, both Congress and the Supreme Court have supported a trend towards cooperation between state and federal authorities. The general rule that the Supreme Court appears to follow is that:

> . . . where the (state) statute regulates evenhandedly to effectuate a legitimate state interest and the effects on commerce are only incidental, it will be upheld unless the burden imposed on such commerce is clearly excessive in relation to the putative local benefits.[21]

Prior to the passage of the Coastal Zone Management Act there was no specific mechanism or process for accommodating distributions of authority in coastal waters as new issues emerged. Previously, most disputes were settled in the courts. However, the state coastal management programs now provide a method of negotiating and formalizing a distribution of power and authority. Congress has declared that the states, using their full authority, are the best points for establishing a national program of coastal zone management.

It is possible that in the future Congress may alter the current balance of power between federal and state interests, or that court decisions will further expand the concept of federal supremacy or preemption. It can be concluded, especially when dealing with coastal waters, that it is not just empty rhetoric to assert that any successful coastal water management and planning effort will require a partnership of both federal and state interests, since under current law neither source has full or sufficient power to unilaterally establish a comprehensive management system.

STATE AUTHORITY UNDER THE COASTAL ZONE MANAGEMENT ACT

The Coastal Zone Management Act establishes a delicate balance of power. The states, rather than the federal government, are to establish comprehensive coastal management programs, including an identification of permissible uses, areas of particular concern, and general principles for development and protection. However, in establishing such plans, the states must consider the national interest, which now explicitly includes the development of energy resources.

Federal authorities are required to assist the states in these planning and management efforts to the maximum possible extent. But state programs are subject to federal review and comment prior to final approval. In addition, states are explicitly prohibited from diminishing the authority of federal agencies. However, federal licenses are not to be granted without a certification that the proposed activity will be consistent with approved state coastal management programs. It is a complex network of checks and balances that will be involved in any major coastal water management decision, and it may represent an unrealistic distribution of authority, with neither the states nor federal agencies having sufficient control to effectively manage the territorial sea.

As described earlier, Congress and the federal courts have often supported federal over state interests in coastal water jurisdictional disputes. The principal logic for federal supremacy has been a perceived need for a uniform national system of regulations in issues related to commerce or navigation. The Rivers and Harbors Act of 1898 and the more recent Ports and Waterways Safety Act establish a partial federal preemption of state control of surface activities.

New Objectives and New Authority

The thrust of past federal coastal water regulations has been centered on three issues: (a) regulation of oil and gas extraction from submerged lands; (b) protection of the navigational characteristics of coastal waters; and most recently, (c) improvement in and protection of water quality.

The Coastal Management Act of 1972 represents a new idea that is in many ways inconsistent with prior legislation and with previous concepts of federal supremacy. Incorporating concepts of multiple use which emerged during the 1960s, the CZMA attempts to combine and reevaluate programs of water quality and surface water traffic management. It advocates a comprehensive approach that looks at the submerged lands, the water column, the surface waters, the air above and the adjacent land as a connected whole. The ultimate objective is to facilitate a wide variety of human activities while assuring the continued viability of the natural marine system.

Rules of federal supremacy that may allow federal control of navigation or commerce to override state attempts at comprehensive coastal resource planning and management are not only counter to the articulated objectives of the Coastal Zone Management Act, but could actually preclude state success in determining and then assuring "wise use" of coastal resources.

Supremacy may lead to the advancement of single-purpose objectives over the comprehensive approach called for in the CZMA. There are major federal programs for the control of dredge and fill, of ocean dumping, of vessel traffic control and of water quality. Yet each of these lacks a broader context within which long-range objectives can be formulated. It is the coastal zone program, with an interconnected set of objectives, priorities and restrictions that can allow a national coordination of these programs. Yet the single element most likely to diminish the impact of this approach is the supremacy doctrine and federal powers associated with the commerce clause of the Constitution.

The control of surface water activities may be more important for managing the marine environment than for purposes of navigation. Encouraging commercial use of the coastal zone is important, as recognized in the CZMA, but commerce is only one of several important uses of coastal waters, and commerce may need to be regulated to allow other uses or to protect the long-range survival of the natural marine ecosystem.

The problem is perhaps potential rather than immediate. But the potential is strong, and should be of considerable concern to state coastal managers. Under the Coastal Zone Management Act, Congress recognizes the state as the best level of government for developing a comprehensive coastal zone management program. Yet the authority of the state is subservient to broad, yet ill-defined concepts of commerce powers and federal supremacy. When efforts at cooperation are made, it is possible that states will be able to effect coordinated comprehensive programs. Yet the Federal Code contains an extensive mandate for federal rather than state control of water activities, especially as they relate to navigation. Chapters 4-10 further describe the present degree of federal authority, and the degree to which it may preclude effective state management programs.

An Example

On February 22, 1977, the Tanker Safety Act of 1977 was introduced in the House, as a set of amendments to the Ports and Waterways Safety Act of 1972 (see also Chapter 8). This legislation would authorize and, in some instances, require the Secretary of Transportation to establish vessel traffic systems, including computerized tracking and data retrieval equipment and comprehensive regulation. Since such control systems could have major impact upon all coastal water users, the Secretary, in Section 103, would be required to take into account a broad variety of factors in establishing rules and regulations. It is significant that *no mention* is made of an approved state coastal zone management program as one of the things the Secretary must consider. It is not clear what, if any, authority states would have over the establishment and implementation of these systems that would control all surface vessel traffic in and near major ports and waterways. The consistency provisions of Section 307 of the CZMA may allow some degree of state participation, but unless this type of legislation begins to take into account the existence of state coastal management programs, state management efforts may be diluted.

CONCLUSIONS

As the use of coastal waters and their resources increased, so did the need to develop more precise specifications of state and federal authority. This task has not been completed, and more disputes between state and federal authority, as well as between public and private interests, can be expected.

However, the Coastal Zone Management Act provides a framework for comprehensive planning, management and coordination that did not exist during earlier disputes. The CZMA has not resolved all questions of jurisdiction, and has perhaps avoided some critical issues which will eventually require resolution. The Act does provide a new mechanism for structured resolution that could benefit both federal and state interests. The effectiveness of the Act will be somewhat limited until there is a similar comprehensive mechanism for the ocean waters beyond the three-mile limit. Within the territorial sea, states have a very real, if constrained, opportunity to orchestrate wise use of coastal waters.

REFERENCES

1. Bartley, E. R. *The Tidelands Oil Controversy,* University of Texas Press, 1953.
2. Engler, R. *The Politics of Oil* pp. 86-95.
   Bartley, E. R. *The Tidelands Oil Controversy.*
   Solberg, C. *Oil Power.* Chapter six.
3. "Submerged Lands Act." Report of the Committee on Interior and Insular Affairs, U.S. Senate, 83rd Congress, Ist Session (1953), p. 37.
4. *The Politics of Oil,* p. 89.
5. Special master's report to the U.S. Supreme Court on *U.S. v. Maine et al.,* August 27, 1974 (Nautilus Press, Inc.).
6. "Coastal Zone Management Act of 1972," Section 304(1) as amended.
7. Office of Coastal Zone Management, Threshold Paper Number One, Boundaries (May 24, 1976), p. 3.
8. Wroth, L. K. "Federal Power as a Limit Upon State Control of Marine Resources," in *Maine Law Affecting Marine Resources,* Volume 4.
   Power, G. *Chesapeake Bay in Legal Perspective,* Part Two.
   Office of Technology Assessment. "Federal and State Regulations of the Three Offshore Energy Technologies," Working Paper #1, Volume II, *Coastal Effects of Offshore Energy Systems.*
   DuBey, R. A. *Control of Oil Transport in the Coastal Zone.*
9. Power, G. *Chesapeake Bay in Legal Perspective,* p. 137.
10. *Ibid.,* p. 131.

11. *U.S. v. Ashland Oil and Transportation Company,* 504 F2d 1317 1320 (6th Cir. 1974).
12. *United States v. Appalachian Power Company,* 311 U.S. 377, 426 (1940).
13. *U.S. v. Wrightwood Dairy Company,* 314 U.S. 110 (1941).
14. Wroth, L. K. *Maine Law Affecting Marine Resources,* Vol. 4, p. 848.
15. Power, G. *Chesapeake Bay in Legal Perspective,* pp. 139-140.
16. *Perez v. Brownell,* 356 U.S. 44, 57 (1958).
17. 1 Stat. 76-77, 28 U.S. C.A. Sec. 1333 (1970).
18. Wroth, L. K. *Maine Law Affecting Marine Resources,* Vol. 4, pp. 868-889.
19. *Kossick v. United Fruit Co.,* 365 U.S. 731 (1961).
20. *Florida Lime and Avocado Growers, Inc. v. Paul,* 373 U.S. 132.
21. *Pike v. Bruce Church, Inc,* 397 U.S. 137, 142 (1970).

RECOMMENDED READINGS

Bartley, E. R. *The Tidelands Oil Controversy* (University of Texas Press, 1953).

Congressional Research Service. *Legislative History of the Coastal Zone Management Act of 1972, as Amended in 1974 and 1976 with a Section-by-Section Index.* National Ocean Policy Study (December, 1976).

Power, G. *Chesapeake Bay in Legal Perspective.* U.S. Department of Interior (March, 1970).

Special Masters Report to the U.S. Supreme Court on U.S. v. Maine, et al., (Nautilus Press, Inc., August 27, 1974).

Wroth, L. K. "Federal Power as a Limit Upon State Control of Marine Resources" in *Maine Law Affecting Marine Resources,* Vol 4 (University of Maine School of Law, 1969).

The state of Washington, as part of the preparation of a coastal management guidebook, has developed a major legal analysis on local, state and federal authorities that was scheduled for completion by July of 1977.

CHAPTER 3

FEDERAL LAWS AND AGENCIES
RELATED TO COASTAL WATERS

FEDERAL LAWS

Many federal laws, programs, rules, policies and regulations affect coastal waters. The problem and challenge for state coastal management programs is to assimilate this diverse collection of federal legislation and agency rules into a cohesive coastal water management system within the territorial waters of each state.

A full discussion of all of the federal laws that might affect coastal management is beyond the scope of this effort. Only the major laws are presented, and many of these may undergo significant revision in the near future. The subject of coastal and ocean management has become the focus of both congressional and executive branch action, and those involved in coastal zone management should be cognizant of pending amendments and reorganizations.

The summaries included in this chapter are not intended as exhaustive discussions of the present legislation. Actual reference to the text of a specific law is strongly recommended (see also Chapter 2).

The following are federal laws affecting coastal water management:

- Clean Air Act
- Deepwater Port Act
- Endangered Species Act
- Federal Aviation Act of 1958
- Federal Water Pollution Control Act
- Fishery Conservation Act

- Intervention on the High Seas Act
- Marine Mammals Protection Act
- Marine Protection, Research and Sanctuaries Act
- Marine Resources and Engineering Development Act
- Military Public Lands Withdrawals Act
- National Environmental Policy Act
- Outer Continental Shelf Lands Act
- Ports and Waterways Safety Act
- Proclamation 2732 of 31 May, 1947
- Rivers and Harbors Act of 1899
- Water Resources Planning Act

Clean Air Act (42 U.S.C. 1857-1857F)

This Act establishes a national program of air quality research, maintenance and improvement. National primary and secondary standards are established, for both point and nonpoint sources of pollution. The Environmental Protection Agency establishes standards which states administer. States are allowed to designate areas as being either Class I, Class II or Class III, which in effect are air quality zones of decreasing restrictiveness.

This is a major federal law which continues to be a source of controversy and amendment. The standards of the law are required by the Coastal Zone Management Act to be the air quality standards for a state coastal management program.

Importance for State Coastal Water Management Programs

The importance of this Act for coastal zone management could be immense. Air loading of coastal waters may be a major source of pollutants such as PCBs, and state coastal management programs may increasingly attempt to use the consistency provisions to insure that state and national air quality standards under the Clean Air Act are consistent with coastal management objectives.

Stringent air quality standards may also determine patterns of coastal water use. It is possible that some activities may seek a coastal water location to use some of its air quality capacity, as compared to major urban land areas. State consideration of priority uses for coastal waters should consider the air quality impacts of various alternatives, as well as other factors such as water dependency.

Deepwater Port Act of 1974 (33 U.S.C. 1501-1524 (1975))

This Act establishes jurisdictional authority over the licensing and regulation of deepwater ports beyond the territorial sea (coastal waters) of the United States.

1. The Secretary of Transportation is authorized to issue licenses for the ownership, construction and operation of deepwater ports. The Secretary must find that the project is consistent with the national interest, national security, and other national policy goals and objectives, including energy sufficiency and environmental quality (Section 4 (c) (3)).

2. The deepwater port must use best available technology so as to prevent or minimize adverse impact on the marine environment (Section 1 (c) (5)).

3. The Environmental Protection Agency must clarify that the deepwater port will conform with all applicable provisions of the Clean Air Act, the Federal Water Pollution Act, and the Marine Protection, Research and Sanctuaries Act (Section 4 (c) (6)). *A license cannot be granted if the governor of any "adjacent" coastal state does not approve* (Section 9 (b) (1)). Adjacency is determined by:

   (a) direct connection by pipeline to the deepwater port;

   (b) being within 15 miles of the deepwater port site; and

   (c) if the Secretary of Transportation, in response to a coastal state's request, designates such a state as an adjacent coastal state.

   This determination is to be based on whether there is a risk of damage to the coastal environment of such state:

   > "equal to or greater than the risk posed to a state directly connected by pipeline to the proposed deepwater port." (Section 9 (a)).

4. If a governor of an adjacent coastal state declares that the application for license is *inconsistent* with state programs relating to environmental protection, land and water use, and coastal zone management, any license granted must be *conditioned* so as to make it consistent with such programs (Section 9 (b) (1)).

5. An oil discharge liability is also established by this Act, including the creation of a $100,000,000 Deepwater Port Liability Fund to be financed by a fee of two cents per barrel for loading or unloading at the deepwater port (Section 18).

6. *The law of the nearest adjacent coastal state will apply to any deepwater port licensed under the Act,* so long as state law is *consistent with federal law* and the regulations of the Deepwater Port Act (Section 19 (b)).

Importance for State Coastal Water Use Management Programs

1. An adjacent coastal state has veto power over the development of any deepwater port.

2. The Coastal Zone Management Act requires that approved state programs reflect a full consideration of the national interest which specifically includes consideration of energy-related facilities. Further, deepwater ports may represent an environmentally superior alternative to increased levels of smaller tankers moving in and out of shore-based ports. Whether this is always true, deepwater ports represent a major regional and national interest and will probably affect most coastal states. Chapter 7 provides further information.

Endangered Species Act of 1973 (16 U.S.C. 1531-1543)

The Secretary of Interior is to prepare a list of endangered species and issue necessary regulations to provide for their conservation. All federal departments and agencies are to insure that "actions authorized, funded, or carried out by them do not jeopardize the continued existence of such endangered species and threatened species or result in the destruction or modification of habitat of species determined by the Secretary to be critical" (Section 7).

Importance for State Coastal Water Management

The full implications of this Act are not clear, and there is growing pressure to modify its provisions. However, it may be of considerable importance, as evidenced by two recent examples:

1. *Tellico Dam Project.* On January 31, 1977, the U.S. Court of Appeals of the Sixth Circuit enjoined the Tennessee Valley Authority from further construction of its almost-completed $116 million Tellico Dam project on the Little Tennessee River. This action was based on the discovery that part of the proposed Tellico Reservoir to be formed by the proposed dam would destroy the habitat of the *snail darter,* a three-inch member of the perch family. The snail darter is on the federal endangered species list because the Little Tennessee River is the sole habitat of the fish (*New York Times,* February 6, 1977).

2. *Dickey-Lincoln Hydroelectric Dam.* In the fall of 1976 a rare
species of wildflower, the furbish lousewort, was discovered
near the Upper St. John River in Maine. This flower has been
proposed for inclusion on the federal endangered species list.
Unless some way can be found of transplanting and protecting
the species, the large hydroelectric dam project, which would
flood and destroy both the specimens and their habitat, may
have to be modified to meet the requirements of the Endangered Species Act.

Federal Aviation Act of 1958

The Secretary of Transportation is authorized and directed to
formulate policy with respect to the use of the navigable airspace,
and assign by rule, regulation or order the use of the navigable airspace under such terms, conditions and limitations as he may deem
necessary to ensure the safety of aircraft and the efficient use of such
airspace. Full consideration must be given to the requirements of
national defense.

Executive Order 10854 of 1959 extended this authority to areas
of land or water outside the United States and the overlying airspace
thereof over or in which the federal government of the United
States appropriate jurisdiction or control, "provided the Secretary of
Defense agrees that it is not inconsistent with the requirements of
national defense."

Importance for State Coastal Water Management Programs

This is the authority through which the Department of Defense
secures various special use airspace designations, and would appear
to constitute a permit under Section 307 (c) (3) (A) of the Coastal
Zone Management Act of 1972, as amended.

Federal Water Pollution Control Act (PL 92-500)

This Act establishes as *national goals* some rather explicit water
quality conditions which could have considerable impact upon
coastal water use decisions.

Section 101(a). The objective of this act is to restore and maintain
the chemical, physical and biological integrity of the nation's waters.

Section 101(a) (1). "It is the national goal that the discharge of pollutants into the navigable waters be eliminated by 1985."

Section 101(a) (2). "It is the national goal that wherever attainable, an interim goal of water quality which provides for the protection and propagation of fish, shellfish, and wildlife and provides for recreation in and on the water be achieved by 1983."

Section 101(a) (3). "It is the national objective that the discharge of toxic pollutants in toxic amounts be prohibited."

Importance for State Coastal Water Management Programs

The amendments of 1972 serve as the source of water quality management for coastal waters, as specified in Section 307(f) of the Coastal Zone Management Act.

Notwithstanding any other provision of this title, . . . the Federal Water Pollution Control Act, as amended . . . *shall* be incorporated in any program developed pursuant to this title and *shall* be the water pollution control . . . requirements applicable to such program. (emphasis added)

Several sections of the Act are important to coastal water use management. Program managers should become familiar with each of the Act's many provisions, including construction grants for sewage treatment systems, and Section 208 areawide waste treatment management plans. A brief summary of some of the sections that have direct impact upon coastal water management follows.

Areawide Waste Treatment Management Plans: Section 208 of the FWPCA provides for regional water quality planning. Many states are approaching such programs as land use planning, and the language of the Act in Section 208 reflects that thinking. However, coastal managers may wish to explore the degree to which 208 funds and provisions might be used for coastal water areas that have "substantial water quality control problems." Perhaps water areas that are subjected to heavy boat traffic, storm water discharge, surface runoff, or similar pollution pressures might be designated as water areas of particular concern, and be managed under Section 208.

Section 311: Oil and Hazardous Substance Liability:
Section 311(b) (1) ". . . it is the policy of the United States that there should be no discharges of oil or hazardous substances into or

upon the navigable waters of the United States, adjoining shorelines, or into or upon the waters of the contiguous zone."

Section 311(c) (2) calls for the creation of a National Contingency Plan for oil spills, including formation of strike forces, and a national center for coordination.

Section 311(o) (2) "Nothing in this section shall be construed as preempting any state or political subdivision thereof from imposing any requirements or liability with respect to the discharge of oil or hazardous substance into any waters within such state."

Section 311(o) (3) "Nothing in this section shall be construed . . . to affect any state or local law not in conflict with this section."

Section 312: Marine Sanitation Devices: to prevent the discharge of untreated or inadequately treated sewage into or upon the navigable waters.

Section 316: Thermal Discharge: to assure the protection and propagation of a balanced indigenous population of shellfish, fish and wildlife.

Section 318: Aquaculture: The Administrator of EPA is authorized to allow certain "pollutant" discharges from approved aquaculture projects.

Section 401: Certification: Any project that will cause a water discharge must obtain a state certification that the activity meets requirements of the Act.

Section 401(c): The Corps of Engineers is authorized to permit use of dredge spoil disposal areas.

Section 402: National Pollutant Discharge Elimination System (NPDES)

Section 403: Ocean Discharge Criteria: Special guidelines are to be promulgated for Section 402 permits that involve the *territorial* sea, the waters of the contiguous zone, or the oceans.

Section 404: Permits for Dredged or Fill Material: Authorizes the Army Corps of Engineers to issue permits for the discharge of dredged or fill material into navigable waters at specified disposal sites.

Section 405: Disposal of Sewage Sludge: Prohibits sludge disposal except under EPA permit. States can request administration of such permits within their jurisdiction.

Section 504: Emergency Powers: The Administrator of EPA can seek court action to restrain any activity that presents "an imminent and substantial endangerment to the health of persons or to the welfare of persons where such endangerment is to the livelihood of such persons, such as inability to market shellfish."

Section 510: State Authority: The states may not adopt or enforce standards which are less stringent than those formulated under the Act. Except as expressly provided in the Act, nothing in the Act shall be construed as impairing or in any manner affecting any right or jurisdiction of the states with respect to the waters (including boundary waters) of such states.

Intervention on the High Seas Act (33 U.S.C. 1471-1487 (1970))

Whenever a ship collision, stranding, or other incident of navigation or the occurrence on board a ship or external to it leads to "a grave and imminent danger" to the coastline or related interests of the United States due to pollution or threat of pollution of the sea by oil, the Secretary of Transportation may take measures on the high seas beyond the coastal waters to prevent, mitigate or eliminate that danger.

Specific coastal resources to be protected include, but are not limite to, fish, shellfish and other living marine resources, wildlife, *coastal zone* and estuarine activities, and public and private shorelines and beaches.

A controlling factor in determining when action can take place is whether or not a "major harmful consequence" is involved. Any remedial actions taken must be limited proportionately to the actual damage that is expected, and such action cannot go beyond what is "reasonably necessary" to prevent, mitigate or eliminate that damage.

Importance for State Coastal Water Management Programs

While states do not have jurisdiction beyond the territorial sea, they could seek DOT assistance under authority of this Act to take action on a hazard threatening state coastal waters.

Marine Mammals Protection Act (16 U.S.C. 1361; 1371-1384)

The taking, importing, exchanging, selling or trading of marine mammals requires a permit. With some exceptions, killing of marine mammals is prohibited. A Marine Mammal Commission is established and is administered by Interior's Fish and Wildlife and by the National Marine Fisheries Service of NOAA.

Importance for State Coastal Water Management Programs

This Act establishes another *national interest* which state coastal management programs are required to consider. The greatest impact to date has been upon the tuna fishing industry, requiring the protection of porpoise (see Chapters 5 and 11). The protection of marine mammals and of marine mammal habitats within territorial waters thus becomes an important part of coastal water use management and warrants consideration as a designated priority use of coastal waters.

The Act also provides assistance to states to establish research and protection programs, and allows state administration under federal supervision. These provisions might serve as technical and financial support for coastal water planning and management efforts.

Marine Protection, Research and Sanctuaries Act of 1972 (33 U.S.C. 1401-1444)

See Chapter 4.

Marine Resources and Engineering Development Act of 1966 (33 U.S.C. 1101-1108)

This Act establishes the National Council on Marine Resources and Engineering Development charged with coordinating federal marine science research and development. It also authorized the establishment of a Commission on Marine Science, Engineering and Resources which prepared *Our Nation and the Sea,* a report that still serves as an excellent description of national coastal management issues and opportunities.

Importance for State Coastal Water Management Programs

Our Nation and the Sea remains a valuable source of information and warrants review by those interested in coastal water management. The National Council, composed of the chiefs of major federal departments, could serve an important role in the formation of a national ocean policy, and in resolving some of the present jurisdictional conflicts within the territorial sea. However, its linkage with the national coastal zone management program is unclear and some agencies seem unsure as to its value or future.

Military Public Lands Withdrawal Act (43 U.S.C. 155-158)

This Act stipulates that an act of Congress will be necessary for the withdrawal of public lands, including those of the outer continental shelf, for purposes of national defense, if such withdrawals would involve more than 5000 acres.

Importance for State Coastal Water Management Programs

This is not the most significant of federal acts relating to national security and coastal water use management. However, it serves to call attention to the extremely complex issues of limited and unlimited national emergencies under which the Executive Office of the President has, over the past 30 years, established several rules related to national defense. Many of these rules are still in effect, and during times of future national emergencies, under present law, the Office of the President is given extraordinary powers to establish orders such as the declaration of security areas in coastal or ocean waters. During time of war, these powers, as well as those of Congress, are expanded by another order of magnitude.

For most coastal states, there is no immediate need to explore rules promulgated under past or still-declared national emergencies, or under war powers. But it is of importance to recognize that most of the provisions of the Coastal Zone Management Act could be seriously affected under national emergency or war conditions. The implications of this are not always obvious and deserve consideration.

National Environmental Policy Act of 1969 (42 U.S.C. 4321-4347)

This Act established the Council on Environmental Quality and the requirements for the now familiar Environmental Impact Statement (EIS) to be prepared for every significant federal project. What must be contained in an EIS has expanded to the point where most EIS's are significant decision documents and important sources of management information. Federal agencies are allowed to make an initial determination of when an EIS is required.

Importance for State Coastal Water Management Programs

This law has two impacts upon state management programs. First, it serves as a useful source of information. For example, the New Hampshire Coastal Management Program has obtained a significant amount of its inventory data from federal EIS's, such as that prepared for the Seabrook nuclear power plant. Without such information, states might be unable to assess the degree of consistency of a proposed activity.

Secondly, NEPA establishes a requirement, under law, that environmental impact be taken into consideration. If a major adverse impact will result from a project, that impact must be identified and evaluated. Failure to prepare a proper impact statement can lead to the blockage of a project. A measure of this potential can be found in the January 17, 1977, action of Federal Judge Weinstein. He ruled the major mid-Atlantic OCS lease of 93 tracts made in August of 1976 as being null and void (*Wall Street Journal,* February 18, 1977). The basis of his action was that the EIS for the lease was inadequate, having failed to consider several important factors such as the potential ability of local communities to block landfalls of OCS pipelines.

NEPA can be used as a positive tool to gather otherwise unavailable information, and to force activity sponsors to focus upon the critical task of using coastal waters in such a way as to minimize destruction or disruption.

Outer Continental Shelf Lands Act (43 U.S.C. 1331-1343 (1964))

Historically, this Act is a companion piece to the Submerged Lands Act of 1953 (see Chapter 2). It establishes federal jurisdiction, control and power over the subsoil and seabed of the outer continental shelf. This not only adopts the Truman Proclamation which extended U.S. jurisdiction beyond three miles, but also makes quite clear that beyond three miles federal, rather than state, authority is to control the submerged lands.

This act is of considerable importance, since, along with the Submerged Lands Act, it is the basic source of state authority in coastal waters. Several proposals for modification of this Act have been made in recent years, a frequent feature of which has been to allow more state participation in federal leasing decisions.

The right to navigation and fishing and, in general, to activities other than submerged lands activities, are not affected by the Act. This is the basic authority for the Department of the Interior to lease OCS lands. It also established that the Federal Power Commission shall regulate gas pipelines and that the Interstate Commerce Commission shall regulate oil pipelines.

The OCSLA states that the criminal and state laws of the state directly inshore from any artificial islands apply to "artifical islands and fixed structures," as well as to the submerged lands of the outer continental shelf. But if state law is to apply, it must be consistent with federal laws and regulations (Section 4(a) (2)).

U.S. District Courts are given original jurisdiction of cases and controversies involving:

> " . . . exploring for, developing, removing or transporting by pipeline the natural resources, or involving rights to the natural resources of the subsoil and seabed of the outer continental shelf . . . ." (Section 4(b)).

The Secretary of the Interior is authorized to cooperate with the conservation agencies of adjacent states (Section 5(a) (1)).

In the event of a controversy between the United States and a state as to whether or not lands are subject to the provisions of this Act, the Secretary is authorized to negotiate with the state in questions regarding operations of leases, payments and the issuance of new leases.

Section 8(a) speaks of the "urgent need" for further exploration and development of the oil and gas deposits of the submerged lands of the outer shelf.

Section 8(c) suggests that there is an "urgent need" for exploration and development of sulfur deposits in the submerged lands of the outer continental shelf.

Section 11 allows for the geological and geophysical exploration in the outer continental shelf, as authorized by the Secretary, but only if they are "not unduly harmful to aquatic life in such area."

The Secretary of Defense, with the approval of the President, can restrict from exploration and operation any portions of the outer continental shelf "needed for national defense" (Section 12(d)).

Importance for State Coastal Management Programs

This is a key piece of legislation and it is recommended that each state program manager become familiar with its provisions. Further, it is suggested that each state coastal zone management program attempt to keep track of pending congressional modifications of this law.

There remain serious questions as to how the Coastal Zone Management Act may affect the provisions of this law. For example, the Office of Coastal Zone Management threshold papers explicitly prohibit the inclusion of OCS waters or submerged lands within the boundaries of an approved coastal zone management program. Yet the Act establishes as a basic objective the formation of state programs that regulate direct and significant impacts upon coastal waters. Of critical importance in terms of jurisdiction is that OCS developments, while outside the coastal zone, may be major sources of direct and significant impacts upon coastal waters. To the degree that a state can establish that activities occurring under the jurisdiction of the Outer Continental Shelf Lands Act will impart a direct and significant impact upon their state coastal waters, they may be able to establish some claim to a need for federal consistency within an approved CZM program as a criterion in the administration of the OCSLA.

This is a sensitive issue which could lead to future disputes between state and federal interests. However, the state is in a strong position to influence and to some degree control OCS activities.

Most if not all of these activities are at some point dependent upon coastal waters or shorelands, both of which fall within the administrative jurisdiction of coastal states (see Chapter 10 for discussion of this point).

**Ports and Waterways Safety Act of 1972
(33 U.S.C. 1221-1227 (1970))**

The purpose of this Act is to promote the safety of ports, harbors, waterfront areas and navigable waters of the United States. The Secretary of Transportation is authorized to establish vessel traffic systems, methods of vessel operation, and standards of vessel equipment and construction.

Section 104 requires the Secretary of Transportation to provide an "adequate opportunity" for states to consult and comment upon proposed rules, regulations and standards.

Section 102(c) provides that the Secretary may consider, utilize and incorporate regulations or similar directory materials issued by port or other state and local authorities.

Section 102(b) allows states to establish higher equipment requirements or safety standards:

> " . . . nor does it prevent a state or political subdivision thereof from prescribing for structures only higher safety equipment requirements or safety standards than those which may be prescribed pursuant to this title."

Importance for State Coastal Water Management Programs

This Act provides the Coast Guard with considerable authority to regulate vessel traffic in coastal waters and to establish regulations for tanker safety. At issue is the degree to which this Act preempts state authority. The U.S. Supreme Court has agreed to consider this and associated issues resulting from a challenge to Washington State's tanker regulations.

Proclamation 2732 of 31 May, 1947 (See 33 U.S.C. Section 143)

This proclamation gives the Department of the Army authority and jurisdiction for the establishment and abandonment of anchorages and restricted areas in navigable waters of the United States and its possessions.

Importance for State Coastal Water Management Programs

This is a principal source of authority by which the Navy establishes its operational areas within the coastal waters of the United States.

Rivers and Harbors Act of 1899 (30 Stat 1151-1153)

This is a primary source of jurisdictional authority for the U.S. Army Corps of Engineers, along with the FWPCA amendments of 1972.

Section 9: Within state coastal waters, the Corps must approve plans for the constructions of any bridge, dam, dike, or causeway.

Section 10: Unless approved by Congress, any obstruction to the navigable capacity of any of the waters of the United States is prohibited. Also:

(a) outside of established "harbor lines" (bulkhead lines), the Corps must approve the construction of any wharf, pier, dolphin, boom, weir, breakwater, bulkhead, jetty, or other structure in any port, roadstead, haven, harbor, canal, navigable river, or other water of the United States; and

(b) within the limits of an established harbor line, Corps approval is needed to excavate or fill, or in any manner to alter or modify the course, location, condition, or capacity of any port, roadstead, haven, harbor, canal, lake, harbor of refuge, or enclosure, or of the channel of any navigable water of the United States.

Section 11: The Secretary of War is granted the power to establish harbor lines, beyond which no piers, wharves, bulkheads or other works shall be extended or deposits made except under regulations which the Secretary may establish.

Section 13: A permit system administered by the Secretary of War and the Chief of Engineers is established. Without a permit it is unlawful to throw, discharge or deposit, or cause, suffer or procure to be thrown, discharged or deposited either from or out of any ship, barge or other floating craft of any kind, or from the shore, wharf, manufacturing establishment or mill of any kind, any refuse matter of any kind or description whatever other than that flowing from streets and sewers (regulated now by FWPCA amendments of 1972) into any navigable water of the United States or into any tributary of any navigable water.

Section 14: It is illegal to deface, remove or tie vessels to public works in coastal waters or to aids to navigation.

Section 15: It is unlawful to tie up or anchor vessels or other craft in navigable channels in such a manner as to prevent or obstruct the passage of other vessels or craft.

Section 20: In an emergency, if a vessel or boat is sinking, grounded or otherwise stopping, seriously interfering with or specially endangering navigation, the Secretary may take immediate possession of the vessel and remove or destroy it to clear canals, locks or navigable waters.

Several of these provisions have been duplicated or transferred through recent legislation. The "ocean dumping" regulations, the Title 33 authorities of the Coast Guard, the Rivers and Harbors Act, and the various provisions of the 1972 amendments of the Federal Water Pollution Control Act are basically expansions of this earlier legislation. This legislation constitutes a powerful jurisdictional foundation for regulation which conflicts with some of the provisions and declared congressional intents of the Coastal Zone Management Act (see Chapter 2). It is also not clear as to how this and similar federal legislation cited above relates to the extensive state regulatory authorities recognized in the Submerged Lands Act of 1953. The degree to which this extensive federal authority might effectively limit state ability to control direct and significant impacts upon coastal waters may be mitigated by the Section 307 consistency requirements of the CZMA. However, there may also be a need for legislative adjustment to explicitly recognize some degree of state authority over the subjects of this Act.

Water Resources Planning Act (42 U.S.C. 1962)

This Act established the Water Resources Council, composed of Secretaries of Interior, Agriculture, Army, HEW and the Chairman of the Federal Power Commission.

The congressional policy statement, in Section 1962, encourages the conservation, development and utilization of water and related land resources of the United States on a comprehensive and coordinated basis by the federal government, states, localities and private enterprise with the cooperation of all affected federal agencies, states, local governments, individuals, corporations, businesss enterprises and others concerned.

Regional river basin commissions were also authorized under this Act. Two of these, the New England River Basin Commission and the Great Lakes Basin Commission, have become active participants in coastal zone planning and management.

Importance for Coastal Water Management Programs

Comprehensive management of water resources has been advocated in one form or another since the mid-1800s, and the Inland Waterways Commission Report of 1908 provides a specific statement of this concept. The Water Resources Planning Act represents a "final" step in a management concept that had been evolving for at least 50 years. But the Water Resources Planning Act and the associated Water Resources Development Act of 1974 (PL 93-251) have little direct connection with comprehensive coastal zone or ocean management. Thus, there are currently two sets of comprehensive water planning efforts, one for inland waters, including river and river basin planning, and another one for coastal zone management. If an ocean policy is ever formulated, there may exist three separate comprehensive water management systems, with little legislative or administrative coordination.

As an example of possible connections, there remains a basic issue as to who should establish quality standards for major river discharges into coastal waters. Are coastal managers to accept present inland water inputs to the coastal waters as a "given" or can they develop concepts of acceptable levels of water quality based upon the uses and tolerances of the coastal zone? At present there is no clear legal or national policy recognition of this type of problem.

FEDERAL AGENCIES ASSOCIATED WITH COASTAL WATER USE MANAGEMENT

The following descriptions are not intended to be comprehensive presentations of the activities and authorities of federal agencies. Some of the more significant and direct programs relating to a state's coastal water use management efforts have been identified and briefly described, but these are not exhaustive.

At this time there is considerable interest in possible changes in the distribution of jurisdictional authority within coastal ocean management. It is quite possible that significant executive branch reorganizations will take place that will have a direct impact upon coastal water use management. Therefore, it is suggested that files be kept on existent and new programs and agencies. The "packet" approach of the state of Washington provides one possible example.

As a further suggestion, state coastal managers may wish to devote time to a detailed study of existent laws and programs at the federal level. While the Coastal Zone Management Act of 1972 provides a principal source of direction and funding for coastal water use planning and management, there are other sources. Considerable opportunities are available for a creative augmentation of state research and enforcement capabilities by fully utilizing these additional programs.

The following federal agencies are concerned with coastal water use management:

- Department of Commerce
- Department of Defense
- Department of Energy
- Department of Health, Education and Welfare
- Department of Interior
- Department of Transportation
- Environmental Protection Agency
- National Aeronautics and Space Administration

Department of Commerce

Principal Coastal Water Legislation

- Coastal Zone Management Act of 1972
- Endangered Species Act
- Fish and Wildlife Coordination Act
- Fishery Conservation Act of 1976
- Marine Mammal Protection Act of 1972
- National Sea Grant College and Program Act of 1966

Some Major Coastal Water Management Agencies and Programs

- National Oceanic and Atmospheric Administration
- Office of Coastal Zone Management
- National Ocean Survey

- Economic Development Administration
- Federal Maritime Administration
- National Marine Fisheries Service
- Sea Grant
- Environmental Data and Information Services

Principal Activities

- Administration of Coastal Zone Management Act of 1972
- Ocean dumpsite monitoring and research, as required under Title II of the Marine Protection, Research and Sanctuaries Act of 1972
- Administration of the Fishery Conservation Act of 1976
- Administration of the National Sea Grant Program
- Administration of the Marine Mammal Protection Act
- Operation of National Environmental Satellite Service
- Operation of Environmental Data and Information Services, including Environmental Data Index (ENDEX) and Oceanic and Atmospheric Scientific Information System (OASIS)
- Operation of National Climatic Center
- Operation of National Oceanographic Data Center
- Operation of National Oceanographic Instrumentation Center
- Research on weather, marine ecosystems, climate modification, aquaculture, anadromous fisheries and fish gear development

Economic Development Administration (EDA)

EDA has the general purpose of providing funds to communities for projects that will improve economic base and unemployment.

As part of this funding, it is estimated that EDA has invested more than $100 million for port facilities since 1965.[1]

EDA is a potential source of funding for coastal water-related development that could have significant impact upon coastal water management programs.

Federal Maritime Administration

Under a mandate derived from the Merchant Marine Act of 1936 and the Merchant Marine Act of 1970, the Maritime Administration attempts to provide a modern efficient U.S. merchant fleet and maintain a strong shipbuilding industry.

The Maritime Administration has provided essential funds for supertankers, LNG carriers and, most recently, nuclear-powered tankers. In fiscal 1975 the Maritime Administration provided oil tanker and LNG carrier subsidies of $275 million per year.

The Maritime Administration maintains the national Merchant Marine Academy at Kings Point, New York,and supports six state merchant marine schools.

The Maritime Administration supports research and development projects on new cargo systems and better construction techniques.

National Marine Fisheries Service (NMFS)

NMFS administers several laws and programs, including the Anadromous Fish Conservation Act, the Endangered Species Act, the Commercial Fisheries Research and Development Act, the Fish and Wildlife Coordination Act, the Fishery Conservation and Management Act, the Fur Sea Act, the Marine Mammal Protection Act and the Marine Migratory Game Fish Act.

NMFS reviews Sections 9, 10, 402 and 404 permits and other federal programs for impact upon fisheries.

NMFS works with the Fish and Wildlife Service (Interior) on many research, review and management tasks related to marine fisheries.

NMFS designates critical marine habitats for endangered species.

NMFS sponsors fisheries research, including marketing, gear testing and habitat improvement.

Department of Defense (DOD)

Department of the Navy

Develops and maintains defense and security capability.

Operates tactical marine systems.

Conducts research on marine weapon systems.

Monitors marine development and usage patterns.

Conducts extensive research in all aspects of the marine environment, including studies of deep ocean bathymetry, marine mammal behavior, coastal hydrographic surveys and underwater acoustics.

Defense Advanced Research Projects Agency

Conducts extensive research and development efforts on a wide variety of concepts and systems with military potential.

U.S. Army Corps of Engineers

Is responsible for primary permit control over hazards to navigation, shoreline construction and dredging, through mandate of Rivers and Harbors Act of 1899, Marine Protection, Research and Sanctuaries Act, Federal Water Pollution Control Act Amendments of 1972 and River and Harbor Act of 1902.

Constructs and maintains harbor and marine facilities.

Conducts research on navigation and coastal engineering (also other areas).

Department of Energy

The Department of Energy (DOE) was created by the passage of the *Department of Energy Organization Act* on August 4, 1977, and became operational October 1, 1977. It can be expected that the Department of Energy will have major impact upon coastal and ocean affairs, not only through the exercise of its present legislative mandate, but also through new advocacy of centralized energy planning.

Federal Energy Regulatory Commission

This independent organization within DOE retains many of the functions of the Federal Power Commission, which includes licensing and regulatory authority over natural gas, including LNG, oil and electric power operations. The FERC also has absorbed the previous authority of the Interstate Commerce Commission to establish rates for transporting oil by pipeline.

Assistant Secretary for Resource Applications

This department will have responsibility for developing commercially available energy supplies. The *strategic oil stockpile* program, which may have considerable long-range coastal impact, is administered by this department.

Assistant Secretary for Energy Technology

This office will direct research into new energy technologies, including ocean-related systems. It will also administer the nuclear fuel cycle waste management program, including research into the *Seabed Emplacement Program*, formerly administered by ERDA, which is seeking an undisturbed environment in which high-level nuclear wastes can be contained for several thousand years.

Assistant Secretary for Environment

This office will prepare EIS's, undertake environmental research and develop environmental policy for DOE.

Department of Health, Education and Welfare (HEW)

Principal Coastal Water Legislation

> Food, Drug and Cosmetic Act (21 U.S.C. 301)

Major Coastal Water Management Agencies and Programs

> Food and Drug Administration
> National Shellfish Sanitation Program
> National Institute of Health

Food and Drug Administration (FDA)

FDA is responsible for insuring that food obtained from the ocean, shipped in interstate commerce, is safe, pure, wholesome and processed under sanitary conditions.

FDA administers the National Shellfish Sanitation Program which is a voluntary federal, state and industry effort to protect and improve the quality of shellfish.

FDA inspects plant inspections and samples the quality of fish and fish products to insure safety and quality.

Department of Interior (DOI)

Bureau of Outdoor Recreation

Distributes funds from Land and Water Conservation Fund Act of 1965, encouraging and assisting in recreational planning.

Bureau of Land Management (BLM)

BLM manages federal submerged lands.
Under authority of Outer Continental Shelf Lands Act, regulates and supervises leasing of OCS lands.
Grants right-of-way permits for common carrier pipelines.

Fish and Wildlife Service

Administers (often with NMFS) Fish and Wildlife Conservation Act, Anadromous Fish Conservation Act, Endangered Species Act, Wildlife Restoration Act, Marine Mammals Protection Act.
Performs marine and environmental studies, federal aid programs for fish and wildlife restoration, technical management assistance, and fishery research. Prepared seven-volume National Estuary Study.

National Park Service

Activities related to coastal water management include administration of National Lakeshores, National Seashores, and coastal recreation areas. These are often focal points for coastal water activities.

U.S. Geological Survey

Administers OCS activities once BLM has leased. (See Chapter 10.)
Extensive research, including identification of possible submerged lands toxic substance disposal sites. (See *Directory of U.S. Geological Survey Program Activities in Coastal Areas 1974-1976* for full description.)

Department of Transportation

Coast Guard

Is the primary law enforcement agency in coastal and ocean waters.
Has enforcement or other responsibilities under Ocean Dumping Act (MPRSA), Dangerous Cargo Act, Ports and Waterways Safety Act, Tanker Act, OCS Lands Act, Fishery Conservation and Management Act, Federal Water Pollution Control Act amendments of 1972.

Conducts marine safety and rescue operations.
Maintains navigation aids including LORAN.
Controls ships in harbors, channels and at deepwater ports.
Is responsible for icebreaking activities.
Maintains land, air and sea patrols.
Distributes *Notice to Mariners* and other publications.
Operates a Pollution Incident Reporting System.
Maintains a strike force and special oil pollution cleanup equipment, as part of *National Contingency Plan* (FWPCA).
Develops standards for design, construction, alteration, repair, maintenance and operation of vessels and deepwater ports.

Office of Pipeline Safety

Establishes and enforces standards necessary to insure safe construction and operation of offshore pipelines used to transport hazardous materials, such as natural gas, petroleum and petroleum products to shore facilities.

Environmental Protection Agency

Principal Legislation

>Federal Water Pollution Control Act
>Clean Air Act
>Marine Protection, Research and Sanctuaries Act

Principal Activities

EPA regulates ocean dumping.
Establishes national air and water quality standards.
Regulates Coastal Water outfalls.
Administrates 208 areawide water quality programs.
Conducts research on spills of oil and hazardous materials, on marine ecosystems and on impacts of activities upon marine environment.

National Aeronautics and Space Administration (NASA)

NASA conducts extensive research on use of remote sensing for development of marine-related research.

Researches application of NASA management techniques to OCS leasing and development regulations.

Is developing SEASAT-A satellite to test remote sensing and data system capabilities to collect information on global marine environment.

REFERENCES

1. Shenker, Eric *et al. The Great Lakes Transportation System,* University of Wisconsin Sea Grant (1976), p. 246.

RECOMMENDED READINGS

Bureau of Coastal Zone Planning. *An Overview of Existing Government Roles and Responsibilities,* State of Florida (January 1977).

Congressional Research Service. *A Compilation of Federal Laws Relating to Conservation and Development of Our Nation's Fish and Wildlife Resources, Environmental Quality, and Oceanography* (Washington, D.C.: U.S. Government Printing Office, 1973).

Department of Energy. *Organization and Functions Fact Book* (September 1977).

General Accounting Office. *Federal Agencies Administering Programs Related to Marine Science Activities and Oceanic Affairs* (February 1975).

Marcus, P. A., Ed. *Directory to U.S. Geological Survey Program Activities in Coastal Areas 1974-1976* (Washington, D.C.: U.S. Government Printing Office, 1976).

National Marine Fisheries Service and U.S. Fish and Wildlife Service. *Living Coastal Resources,* Office of Coastal Zone Management (July 1976).

Office of Technology Assessment. "Federal Laws Relevant to Offshore Development," in *Coastal Effects of Offshore Energy Systems,* Volume II (November 1976), pp. 109-163.

PART 3

COASTAL WATER USES AND ACTIVITIES

INTRODUCTION

Use of coastal and ocean waters is increasing, and the objective of comprehensive coastal water use management is to coordinate these uses in ways that will protect the resource base and minimize user conflicts. Chapters 4-10 describe specific coastal water activities, providing an initial discussion of how these might relate to a state's coastal management program.

These descriptions are introductory in nature: each warrants a full document. An effort has been made to incorporate the most recent legislation and regulations, and in most instances the discussions cover developments through early spring, 1977. However, major changes in either agency regulations or congressional legislation are pending and the entire field of ocean and coastal management is at a point of change. Readers are both cautioned and urged to make direct contact with the agencies and programs identified in these discussions for updated and more complete information.

There are a number of important activities which are not discussed, such as ocean mining, water transportation and marine recreation. The activity profiles described in this chapter are representative of a complex web of human uses and natural systems and are not intended to be inclusive. The activities that have been profiled were chosen not because they are necessarily the most important, but because in total they are more representative of the broad range of problems and opportunities involved in management of coastal waters. Furthermore, each of these activities is already or will soon become a matter of concern for several coastal states,

65

and each of the activities described involves some degree of federal/state jurisdictional complexity. National defense was included not only for these reasons, but also because the authors feel that this important area has not received sufficient attention either in state coastal plans or in the planning literature.

As each activity, with its specific management problems, information needs and federal legislation is examined, the reader is urged to focus on the idea of the attempt to integrate each of these into a single management program. This integration, which has not taken place at the federal level, is both the opportunity and the task of states implementing coastal water management concepts under the Coastal Zone Management Act.

CHAPTER 4

OCEAN DUMPING

Principal Agencies: U.S. Environmental Protection Agency
U.S. Army Corps of Engineers
U.S. Coast Guard
Principal Legislation: Marine Protection, Research and Sanctuaries Act
Federal Water Pollution Control Act
Rivers and Harbors Act of 1899

   Historically, coastal waters have been used for the disposal of a
wide variety of noxious, hazardous or toxic materials. The oceans
and coastal waters have also been routinely used to dispose of
materials such as dredge spoil, which due to sheer bulk represent
major disposal problems in terms of transportation costs and location of acceptable sites. As mentioned in Chapter 1, a major dif-
ference between coastal lands and coastal waters is in the lack of
immediate visibility of the impacts of human use of coastal waters
compared to use of land areas. It is in part because of this that
coastal waters are sought as a site for dumping. Water disposal
frees valuable land for other uses and tends to avoid nuisance or
hazard conditions in major population areas. In most instances, it
also saves a considerable amount of money. Waste is transported
by surface vessel to some coastal water or ocean site and "dumped,"
without concern about burial, further treatment or surface restoration, as is often required for landfill sites.
   The use of coastal waters for waste disposal represents a series of
management issues which will become more complex as coastal water
use increases for a variety of other purposes. In effect, the use of
coastal waters for waste disposal is an allocative decision on how the

assumed assimilative capacity of coastal waters will be used, and consequently how surface, water column and submerged lands shall be used. As recent studies[1,2] and growing conflicts suggest, coastal waters may not have the assimilative capacity that was once assumed and, if such a characteristic does exist, it is not being used properly (see Chapter 5, Case Histories).

Waste disposal within coastal waters includes the use of coastal waters for sewage outfalls, as well as for heat disposal from power plants and other industrial activities. For the purposes of this discussion, waste disposal shall be primarily confined to the more specific activities of "dumping," especially of sewer sludge, dredge spoil, industrial waste or military ordinance.

INCREASE IN OCEAN DUMPING

The use of coastal and ocean waters for the disposal of wastes has greatly increased in recent years. In the early 1950s some 1.7 million tons of industrial wastes, sewage sludge, solid wastes and construction and demolition debris was being dumped into the oceans each year. Added to that were several million tons of dredge spoil. By the mid-1960s this amount had expanded to 7.4 million tons a year, for an estimated increase of 335%.[3] In 1975, over 5 million tons of sludge was dumped into the ocean, along with 3.4 million tons of industrial waste.[4] In 1976 the City of Philadelphia was permitted to dump 120 million pounds of solids and an unlimited amount of liquids as part of its sewage sludge disposal program. This trend should begin to sharply reverse as the Environmental Protection Agency continues its enforcement of the Marine Protection, Research and Sanctuaries Act. In 1976 the amount of waste dumped at sea is estimated by EPA to have declined by almost 600,000 tons. However, even with this reduction, more than 8 million tons of waste was dumped during 1976 into coastal and ocean waters.[5]

The forces that have led to increased ocean dumping help to define the management task facing coastal managers. The Library of Congress, in its study of ocean dumping[2] suggests four primary reasons for dumping increases:

1. There was a widely held perception, which to some degree continues today, that the ocean can serve as a vast ultimate sink for wastes. This view gave rise to the assumption that the ocean was a "safe" disposal site able to dilute and absorb otherwise harmful material.

2. Between 1930 and 1970 the population in coastal areas approximately doubled. This growth of population and associated land development led to the generaiton of tremendous amounts of solid waste. At the same time, this growth reduced the amount of land available for landfill disposal methods.

3. Since the late 1960s there have been growing numbers and types of controls upon air and water discharge. This has led to:

    (a) A transfer of waste disposal processes to coastal and ocean dumping, transferring pollution from one medium to another rather than eliminating it; and

    (b) Pollution controls have themselves expanded the amount of waste needing disposal. Sewage treatment has generated more sewage sludge, and stack scrubbers collect large amounts of fly ash. Both of these are bulky wastes that require some type of disposal.

4. Until 1972 there was no federal regulation of ocean dumping. In many instances this encouraged use of ocean dumping over other methods of waste disposal.[6]

WHAT IS BEING DUMPED

Under the Marine Protection, Research and Sanctuaries Act (MPRSA) a permit is required to dump any material into coastal waters. The Federal Water Pollution Control Act Amendments of 1972 provide additional controls over discharge and also require a permit. Thus, in theory, there is a mechanism for complete inventory and control over what is dumped into coastal and ocean waters.

But to monitor the territorial seas, much less the oceans beyond, is an immense task, and in reality it is probable that ocean dumping is not fully monitored or inventoried. The General Accounting Office (GAO) recently estimated that about one-half of all ocean dumping occurs at night. Yet because of a shortage of personnel and the importance of other missions, the Coast Guard at this time does not conduct night surveillance.[7]

The GAO report also contends that the Coast Guard checks few boats for permits, and that in the 1975 fiscal year less than 1% of

6038 dumpings of substances other than toxic chemicals was actually observed.[8] An electronic Ocean Dumping Surveillance System (ODSS) that would transmit actual vessel location and time of dump from a vessel to district Coast Guard offices is being tested at this time. If successful, it would greatly assist, although not fully solve, the task of 24-hour monitoring of dumping.

Coastal states rarely have the resources to effectively monitor all ocean dumping. Unless and until there is a comprehensive federal monitoring program there can be no assurance that materials are being dumped where they are supposed to, and no accurate information on how much of what is actually entering coast waters.

EFFECT OF DUMPED MATERIALS UPON COASTAL ENVIRONMENT

The Council on Environmental Quality (CEQ) in its 1970 study of ocean dumping,[1] suggested that seven major areas required further research:

1. development of effective national and international pollution monitoring system;
2. development of alternatives to ocean dumping;
3. ecological research on pathways of waste materials in marine ecosystems;
4. preservation and study of representative ecosystems;
5. oceanographic studies of physical and chemical processes;
6. identification of marine pathogens in marine ecosystems; and
7. identification of toxic materials and investigations of the lethal, sublethal and chronic long-term effects of marine life.

According to the 1976 Library of Congress study, "no coherent plan for ocean dumping research exists."[8] Basic questions such as the relative merits of land vs water disposal, or of nearshore vs deep ocean disposal, apparently cannot be answered with any degree of certainty at this time. As EPA officials have testified:

> Locating all disposal sites arbitrarily off the edge of the continental shelf may result in large expenditures which do not achieve environmental benefits. Disposal of some types of waste at such sites may possibly cause greater adverse impact than the use of sites closer to shore. There is no scientific justification at this time for imposing such a restriction on ocean dumping site location.[9]

WHERE TO DUMP

As the above quote indicates, it is not clear at this time what consititues the "best" coastal or ocean dump sites. During 1976 pressure intensified for the relocation of ocean dump sites off the coast of New Jersey into deeper waters, in the hope that greater distance might decrease a growing number of fish kills and beach pollution problems.

Section 102(a) of the Marine Protection, Research and Sanctuaries Act requires the Administrator of EPA, in regulating ocean dumping, to "utilize wherever feasible locations beyond the edge of the continental shelf." This might damage major offshore fishing grounds, such as Georges Bank. Also, such requirements might significantly increase the cost of ocean dumping. To the degree that ocean dumping is a necessary or allowable use, this may be a major consideration. Also, there may be some advantages in allowing dumping closer to shore, even though it might increase the potential for coastal water disruptions:

1. Enforcement of dumping in deep ocean waters may be virtually impossible, due to costs involved.
2. Monitoring, not just for enforcement purposes, but in order to gather more information on coastal water impacts of ocean dumping, may be enhanced at nearshore locations.

WHAT HAS ALREADY BEEN DUMPED AND WHERE IT IS NOW

Until the passage of the MPRSA and the FWPCA, the primary control over ocean dumping was to prevent navigational hazards, under authority of the U.S. Army Corps of Engineers. In most instances permits were not required, and the use of coastal and ocean waters for dumping has in many instances been a principal historic coastal water use. For example, sewage sludge has been dumped at one location in the New York Bight for over 50 years.[10] As Wesley Marx suggests in *The Frail Ocean*, dumping operations must in the future be "charted, plotted, and predicted as carefully as shipping operations."[11]

Examples[1][1]

1. When the Air Force cancelled a Navaho missile contract with North American Aviation Corporation, it advised North American to dump its remaining rocket engines in the ocean. These one-story high structures now represent a hazard to commercial fishing nets and to research vessels dragging expensive test equipment.

2. In 1965, a Texas chemical company dumped 16 drums of sodium oxide residues 20 miles out in the Gulf of Mexico. Seven of the drums returned to shore, propelled by onshore currents, and exploded on the beach in the city of Galveston, Texas.

3. While fishing on the outer banks off North Carolina, Captain Doody of the commercial fishing boat *Snoopy* hauled up a bomb left from a practice bombing run. As another nearby boat reported, there was a terrible blast and "the Snoopy was just gone."[1][2]

4. In 1961, the Collier Chemical and Development Company leased the 40-mile bank off the coast of California from the Department of Interior with the intention of mining deposits of phosphate nodules with a hydraulic dredge. It discovered that there were "unexploded naval projectiles" over large portions of the ocean floor in the lease area, and that the only feasible way of mining was to first remove the unexploded shells. Finding this to be economically prohibitive, the company eventually obtained a refund.

5. In August of 1975, EPA coordinated a survey of the Pacific Farallon Islands 1700-meter (5300 feet) radioactive waste and munitions dump site located some 40 miles west of San Francisco, California. It is estimated that more than 40,000 steel drums filled with concrete in which radioactive waste was mixed and solidified were dumped at this site. Of the containers examined, some showed evidence of hydrostatic implosion and plutonium-238, and plutonium-239, 240 contamination was discovered in the surrounding sediment at levels 2-25 times greater than expected. A similar investigation of the "106-mile site" off the Maryland-Delaware cost, where an estimated 14,000 drums of low-level radioactive waste were dumped from 1951-1962 indicated levels of cesium-137 at concentrations 3-70 times higher than

expected. There is evidence to suggest that the material may be leaching out of the concrete matrix rather than simply leaking from breached containers.[13]

So long as there are materials within or beneath coastal waters which obstruct or endanger other coastal water uses, this heritage from historic patterns of dumping represents a major impediment to increased economic development of coastal resources. In some instances, the probable site of obstacles or hazards can be mapped by tracing through records that public or private agencies might make available. But records may not always exist, or may be difficult to obtain for reasons of security or out of concern over possible liability.

CURRENT REGULATIONS FOR OCEAN DUMPING

At present, there are three basic sources of regulation of ocean dumping:

1. The International Convention on the Prevention of Marine Pollution by Dumping of Wastes and Other Matter
2. The Federal Water Pollution Control Act Amendments of 1972
3. The Marine Protection, Research and Sanctuaries Act of 1972

INTERNATIONAL CONVENTION ON THE PREVENTION OF MARINE POLLUTION BY DUMPING OF WASTES AND OTHER MATTER[1]

This international agreement became effective in August 1975. Formulated in 1972, the Convention establishes a three-part regulatory system.

Annex I ("Black List"): Prohibits dumping of certain substances from vessels, aircraft, platforms or other man-made structures, including high-level radioactive waste and chemical warfare materials.

Annex II ("Gray List"): Requires a special permit to dump heavy metals, cyanides, fluorides, low-level radioactive wastes and other listed materials.

A general permit is required to dump wastes not listed in either Annex I or Annex II.

The Marine Protection, Research and Sanctuaries Act was amended in 1974 to make it more consistent with this Convention, and new regulations[14] issued by EPA for both the MPRSA and the FWPCA attempt to make all three approaches consistent.

THE FEDERAL WATER POLLUTION CONTROL ACT AMENDMENTS OF 1972

As stipulated in Section 307(f) of the Coastal Zone Management Act, this legislation will be the source of all state water quality standards within its coastal management program. Sections 403 and 404 relate specifically to ocean discharge and dumping.

Section 403 (Ocean Discharge Criteria) regulates discharge of nondredged materials from onshore outfall pipes, from all point sources out to 3 miles, and from point sources other than vessels or floating craft out to 12 miles.

Section 404 requires the Environmental Protection Agency to establish regulations for dumping of dredge spoil, and authorizes the Secretary of the Army, acting through the Corps of Engineers, to issue permits for the discharge of dredged or fill material. Regulations for Section 403 are now undergoing extensive revision and coastal managers should watch for them. Regulations for Section 404 of the FWPCA and for the MPRSA were significantly revised by EPA and issued in the Federal Register on January 11, 1977.[15]

MARINE PROTECTION, RESEARCH AND SANCTUARIES ACT (OCEAN DUMPING ACT)

This is a key act for coastal water use management. Title I establishes a basic regulatory mechanism for the control of ocean dumping. Title II requires increased research on ocean dumping. Title III establishes a mechanism for creating Marine Sanctuaries.

Title I of the MPRSA and Section 404 of the FWPCA are administered under regulations published by the U.S. Environmental Protection Agency on January 11, 1977. These regulations establish a comprehensive management system for the control of ocean dumping, and to a large extent have the effect of being the dumping regulations to be used by states in their coastal water use management efforts.

Because alternative methods of waste disposal are difficult and expensive to develop, there has been growing concern that ocean dumping might not end by 1981, even though EPA has established tha date in its regulations. To insure that the 1981 date is met, legislation was introduced in 1977 which would amend the Marine Protection, Research and Sanctuaries Act. Representative of these proposed amendments is H. R. 4297 (May 20, 1977). Section 4(a) of H. R. 4297 requires that:

> The Administrator of the Environmental Protection Agency (here-inafter referred to in this section as the "Administrator") shall end the dumping of sewage sludge into ocean waters, or into waters described in section 101(b) of Public Law 92-532 (MPRSA) as soon as possible after the date of enactment of this section, but in no case may the Administrator issue any permit, or any renewal thereof (under Title I of the Marine Protection, Research and Sanctuaries Act of 1972) which authorizes any such dumping after December 31, 1981.

This bill was signed into law by President Carter in November of 1977. It is not yet clear as to how materials presently being dumped will be disposed of after 1981. Nor is it clear what the costs and possible negative impacts of such alternatives may be. Yet clearly the passage of the Marine Protection, Research and Sanctuaries Act and its 1977 amendments represents a major shift in how coastal and ocean waters are treated.

WHAT CAN BE DUMPED IN COASTAL WATERS

The Environmental Protection Agency (EPA) has stated that its objective is to "eliminate" ocean dumping of unacceptable material as rapidly as possible."[16] The questions of what is possible and what is unacceptable remain issues of great importance, and have been the subject of a law suit brought against EPA by the National Wildlife Federation.

The actual criteria used by EPA in evaluating permit applications is contained in Section 227 of the new regulations. In establishing those criteria, the EPA Administrator is required under Section 102(s) of the MPRSA to consider the following factors:

1. the need for the proposed dumping;
2. the effect of such dumping on human health and welfare, including economic, aesthetic and recreational values;
3. the effect of such dumping on fisheries resources, plankton, fish, shellfish, wildfish, shorelines and beaches;
4. the effect of such dumping on marine ecosystems, particularly with respect to:
   (a) the transfer, concentration and dispersion of such material and its by-products through biological, physical and chemical processes;
   (b) potential changes in marine ecosystem diversity, productivity and stability;
   (c) species and community population dynamics;
5. the persistence and permanence of the effects of the dumping;
6. the effect of dumping particular volumes and concentrations of such materials;
7. appropriate locations and methods of disposal or recycling, including land-based alternatives and the probable impact of requiring use of such alternative locations or methods upon considerations affecting the public interest;
8. the effect on alternative uses of oceans, such as scientific study, fishing and other living resource exploitation and nonliving resources exploitation; and
9. in designating recommended sites, the Administrator shall utilize wherever feasible locations beyond the edge of the continental shelf.

This regulatory system represents a major tool for state coastal water use management, even though its administration is carried out through the Environmental Protection Agency and the Corps of Engineers. EPA is given authority to control dumping over which individual coastal states, through their coastal zone management programs, might not have full control. The burden of issuing permits, monitoring activities and enforcing the law is paid for and administered by federal rather than state agencies. But at the same time, a major portion of coastal water use management is outside direct state control.

STATE AUTHORITY TO REGULATE OCEAN DUMPING

Under the Coastal Zone Management Act, states are encouraged to formulate comprehensive coastal water use management plans that include descriptions of permissible uses, areas of particular concern, and which allow new use of coastal water resources while protecting natural coastal systems and existing uses. As described in Chapter 2, the Submerged Lands Act provides coastal states with a considerable authority over the submerged lands and water resources of the territorial sea. However, that authority is not absolute, and ocean dumping is a particular instance in which Congress appears to have preempted state authority. The Marine Protection, Research and Sanctuaries Act of 1972 is quite specific on this matter. Section 106(d) allows the EPA Administrator to consider suggestions from coastal states, but this is not mandatory, and the states are apparently precluded from regulation of ocean dumping.

> Section 106(d): After the effective date of this title, *no state shall adopt or enforce any rule or regulation relating to any activity regulated by this title.* Any state may, however, propose to the Administrator criteria relating to the dumping of materials into ocean waters within its jurisdiction, or into other ocean waters to the extent that such dumping may affect waters within the jurisdiction of such state, and if the Administrator determines, after notice and opportunity for hearing, that the proposed criteria are not inconsistent with the purposes of this title, may adopt those criteria and may issue regulations to implement such criteria. (emphasis added)

CONSISTENCY

Section 307(c)(1) of the Coastal Zone Management Act, as amended, requires that:

> Each federal agency conducting or supporting activities directly affecting the coastal zone shall conduct or support those activities in a manner which is, to the maximum extent practicable, consistent with approved state management programs.

This would appear to appy to such activities as dredge spoil disposal or the issuance of permits for waste disposal either in coastal waters or in ocean waters to the degree that such dumping would directly and significantly affect coastal waters.

Section 307(c)(3) of the CZMA suggests that EPA could not issue a permit for Ocean Dumping if it were to have a direct and significant impact upon coastal waters and also be inconsistent with a state's program. Designation of dump sites and standards for disposal would also fall under the consistency provisions of the Coastal Zone Management Act.

This federal preemption may represent a major problem. Many coastal states currently have some set of regulations regarding dredge spoil disposal and these may conflict with the prohibitions of the MPRSA. Oregon has recently encountered problems of this sort, and Massachusetts, as described in a following example, may also have future problems. Furthermore, EPA has made an initial claim to the Office of Coastal Zone Management that the Section 106 provisions of the Marine Protection, Research and Sanctuaries Act preempt not only state regulation, but also the consistency provisions of the Coastal Zone Management Act. While it is difficult to sustain such an interpretation of either the Coastal Zone Management Act or the MPRSA, this does indicate that EPA is serious about its authority and that coastal states should carefully examine their present regulations.

However, there is also reason to question the necessity and even the constitutionality of the Section 106 provisions. Congressional adjustment or court declaration may be necessary to clarify this situation. If states were in fact precluded from regulating dumping in either coastal or adjacent ocean waters, they would also be precluded from implementing comprehensive coastal management programs.

DREDGE SPOIL DISPOSAL

The U. S. Army Corps of Engineers is given authority over the regulation of ocean disposal of dredge spoil within coastal waters through Section 103 of the MPRSA and Section 404 of the FWPCA. Through Section 102(a) of the MPRSA, the Environmental Protection Agency also plays an important role in establishing standards.

While ocean disposal of sewage sludge has been confined to the Atlantic coast, the use of coastal or ocean waters for other forms of waste disposal, such as for dredge spoil, is common in all coastal areas. Water disposal of dredge spoil has greatly increased in recent years. As cited in a recent Library of Congress study of ocean dumping, the U.S. Army Corps of Engineers (COE) is increasingly moving towards coastal or ocean dumping rather than land disposal or the use of inland waterways. The reasons are similar to those motivating use of ocean waters for the disposal of other substances:

> "We find that upland areas are no longer available due to the growth of the city surrounding the port; open water disposal in inland areas is being resisted actively by environmental interests...; (and thus, ocean dumping appears the only feasible alternative available to local ports.)"

In 1975, an estimated 87,826,362 cubic yards of dredge spoil was dumped in coastal and ocean waters. There is often an annual variation in amount that depends in part upon available COE funds and upon the degree of flooding or sedimentation that occurs in a given year. If coastal water uses such as recreational and commercial fishing are to increase, more dredging can be anticipated, and with it the need to dispose of more spoil, beyond 1975's total.

If dredge spoil is taken any distance from the site of dredging, major transport costs may be incurred. This can effect a favorable cost-benefit ratio and lead to the rejection of a federally funded maintenance program that could have negative impacts for commercial or recreational uses of coastal waters. And, if improperly dumped, dredge spoil will drift, reclogging channels, burying habitat areas, or otherwise adversely affecting marine resources. Toxic components of dredge spoil could harm living aquatic resources, and the Corps estimates that approximately 34% of the spoil dumped in 1968 was "polluted."

On-land disposal could solve several water-dumping issues, but generates a whole new set of concerns. Included is the possibility that the spoil will leach or wash back into coastal waters. Shore habitat, recreational opportunities, and possible ground water contamination are other concerns that often make land disposal technically, economically or politically difficult.

The Corps may soon discover that as comprehensive water use management programs are developed as part of a state's coastal zone management effort, and as the variety and intensity of coastal water use grows, it may be as difficult to find water disposal sites for dredge spoil as it has become on land. A case in point is the recent Browns Ledge controversy in Massachusetts.

Case History: Browns Ledge, Massachusetts

To improve acess to the harbors of Fall River, Massachusetts, and Providence, Rhode Island, the Corps of engineers has developed channel-deepening projects in Mount Hope and Narrangansett Bays. Previously, Brenton Reef at the mouth of Narrangansett Bay had been used as a spoil-disposal site. Due to opposition which the Corps has identified as being "political and ecological," a new disposal site, Browns Ledge, was designated.

The material to be dumped contains industrial chemicals, oil, gas and heavy metals such as lead and mercury. Browns Ledge serves as a spawning habitat for lobsters, fin and shellfish, and also serves as a migratory station for various finfish. The Corps suggested that tides and currents would tend to prevent toxic elements from settling on the ledge, and offered as a preventive management strategy the imposition of a ban on fishing near the area.

When the Corps held public hearings on its draft environmental impact statement, it received strong opposition from fishermen and other groups. The basic points were that: (a) it appears to some people that the Massachusetts site was chosen because Rhode Island no longer wanted its coastal waters used for dumping; and (b) because of the polluted nature of the dredge spoil, considerable damage might be done to finfish and shellfish stocks, as well as possibly creating a human health hazard if the Browns Ledge site was chosen.

Governor Dukakis of Massachusetts protested by letter to the Corps' regional headquarters in Boston. The governor cited several issues he felt the EIS had not adequately considered, including the possible impacts of heavy metals and chlorinated hydrocarbons on the marine environment and the possible drift of polluted sediments to the Elizabeth Islands and Martha's Vineyard shores during severe storm tides. The Governor concluded by suggesting that the selection of the Browns Ledge site appeared to be primarily an expedient solution based upon political considerations.

The Massachusetts legislature supported the protest by enacting a new state law (Massachusetts General Laws, Chapter 347, Acts of 1976). This law was specifically designed to "effectively negate" the Corps' Browns Ledge proposal. But it also goes beyond that particular issue and establishes a general mechanism for state review and final decision upon proposed waste disposal in Massachusetts coastal waters.

The principal provision of the law is to given the Massachusetts Department of Environmental Quality Engineering exclusive power to issue permits for waste disposal in Massachusetts waters. As of this writing, it is not yet clear how this law will be affected by Section 106(d) of the Marine Protection, Research and Sanctuaries Act of 1972 which states that:

> "After the effective date of this title, no state shall adopt or enforce any rule or regulation relating to any activity regulated by this title. . . ."

Finding an acceptable site for the disposal of large amounts of material, often contaminated in some way, will be increasingly difficult. Yet if coastal water use is to expand, some solutions must be found, since dredging will be an essential adjunct to either recreational or commercial use. If states establish comprehensive management programs for their coastal waters, which include habitat protection, water quality enhancement, and economic development, then perhaps "best" sites for various activities, including dredge spoil disposal, can be more convincingly designated.

REFERENCES

1. Council on Environmental Quality. *Ocean Dumping: A National Policy,* Washington, D. C. (1970).
2. Library of Congress. *Ocean Dumping Regulation: An Appraisal of Implementation,* National Ocean Policy Study, Washington, D. C. (April 1976).
3. Council on Environmental Quality. *Ocean Dumping: A National Policy,* Washington, D. C. (1970), p. 1.
4. National Wildlife Federation. *Conservation Report* (January 28, 1977).
5. Environmental Protection Agency. *Ocean Dumping in the United States: Fifth Annual Report* (1977).
6. Library of Congress. *Ocean Dumping Regulation: An Appraisal of Implementation,* National Ocean Policy Study, Washington, D. C. April 1976), pp. 1,2.
7. *Conservation Report* (January 28, 1977) p. 53.
8. Library of Congress. *Ocean Dumping Regulation: An Appraisal of Implementation,* National Ocean Policy Study, Washington, D. C. (April 1976), p. 74.

9. *Ibid.*, p. 79.
10. *Ibid.*, p. 15.
11. Marx, W. *The Frail Ocean.* (New York: Ballentine, 1969), p. 78.
12. *Ibid.*, p. 77.
13. Environmental Protection Agency. *Ocean Dumping in the United States - 1976.* Washington, D.C. (June 1976), pp. 30-33.
14. *Federal Register* 40 CFR 220-227 (January 11, 1977).
15. Environmental Protection Agency. "Ocean Dumping: Final Revision of Regulations and Criteria, " *Federal Register* (January 11, 1977).
16. *Ibid.*, p. 2462.

RECOMMENDED READINGS

Congressional Research Service. *Ocean Dumping Regulation: An Appraisal of Implementation.* (Washington, D.C.: U.S. Government Printing Office, 1976).

Environmental Protection Agency. "Ocean Dumping: Final Revision of Regulations and Criteria," *Federal Register* (January 11, 1977).

Environmental Protection Agency. *Ocean Dumping in the United States - 1976,* Washington, D.C. (June 1976).

Gross, M. G. *Waste Disposal: MESA New York Bight Atlas Monograph 26.* New York Sea Grant Institute, Albany, New York (July 1976).

This is an excellent report upon dumping in the New York Bight area. It indicates the degree to which historical information can be used to determine what has been dumped, and the variety of inputs to many urban water areas.

CHAPTER 5

FISHERIES MANAGEMENT

Principal Agencies: National Marine Fishery Service (NOAA)
                                    U.S. Fish and Wildlife Service (Interior)
Principal Legislation: Fishery Conservation and Management Act of 1976
                                    Fish and Wildlife Coordination Act
                                    Anadromous Fish Conservation Act
                                    Commercial Fisheries Research and Development
                                        Act of 1964
                                    Marine Mammal Protection Act of 1972

Fisheries and fish stock management have a key role in coastal water use management considerations. Today the United States Consumes some 7 billion pounds (round weight) of fish.[1] This represents a 50% growth in consumption since 1960, and it has been estimated that consumer demand may increase by as much as 2.3 billion pounds (round weight) by 1985[2] leading to an annual consumption level of 9.3 billion pounds. Yet during this period of growing demand for fish products, the United States domestic commercial fishing industry, with the exception of the shrimp, tuna, king crab, salmon and menhaden fleets, has generally remained undeveloped or has deteriorated. Processors have been forced to rely more and more on imports to meet demand.[3]

It is estimated that U.S. coastal waters (within 200 miles) can yield between 20 and 40 billion pounds annually on a sustained basis.[4] But today these waters face a number of pressures, which endanger not only this estimated level of sustained yield, but also threaten the survival of some fish species. For example,

83

while U.S. domestic landings have generally remained at under 5 billion pounds per year (4.7 billion pounds in 1973), the catch of foreign fleets within U.S. coastal waters (including 200-mile zone) has expanded to the point where the foreign catch reached an annual level of 7.9 billion pounds in 1972.[5]

At the present time, there is interest in the establishment of a comprehensive national fisheries management program. Several congressional studies led to the passage of the Fishery Conservation and Management Act of 1976, which created eight regional councils to develop comprehensive fisheries management plans (further description follows). Furthermore, Section 16 of the Coastal Zone Management Act Amendments of 1976 (PL 94-370) required the Secretary of Commerce to undertake a comprehensive review of the molluscan shellfish industry and to present a report to Congress by April 30, 1977. In 1976, the Department of Commerce published *A Marine Fisheries Program for the Nation*, which advocates a six-point national program for fisheries conservation and improvement.

Much attention has been given to the new fishery conservation zone (extended jurisdiction) that went into effect on March 1, 1977. There is considerable hope that this mechanism for controlling foreign fishing pressures within 200 miles of United States shores will protect declining commercial stocks and strengthen the domestic fishing industry. The planning for this zone, under the Fishery Conservation and Management Act of 1976, may represent the first comprehensive national fishery program.

If there is movement towards a national fishery management program, each coastal state is still challenged with major tasks and opportunities within its coastal waters. Much of the prime habitat areas, as well as many of the shore and water activities that can or do conflict with fisheries, are located within the territorial sea.

Control of foreign fishing vessels and the establishment of fishery quotas to insure sustained yield harvesting will be of little long-range value if the quality of coastal waters deteriorates to the point where a healthy fishery cannot be supported. In recent years there has been strong evidence that the living resources of coastal waters are seriously endangered.

PROBLEMS OF POLLUTION

Coastal fisheries are in serious difficulty. This is a result not only of excessive fishing pressures, but also because the coastal waters upon which the fish resources are dependent have in recent years become contaminated with a variety of toxic substances. These substances have either directly killed or damaged the fish stocks, or made finfish and shellfish unfit for human consumption.

In May of 1971, the Food and Drug Administration advised the public to stop eating swordfish, because more than 90% of its samples showed a mercury content of more than 0.5 parts per million (ppm). Although that action by the FDA remains a matter of controversy,[6] it was just the first in a series of pollution-related incidents. A listing of some of these occurences during 1976 and early 1977 indicates the seriousness and complexity of protecting living resources in coastal waters.

1. In 1976, the New York State Department of Environmental Conservation discovered high levels of Mirex and PCBs in Lake Ontario. In September of 1976, the state warned Lake Ontario fishermen not to eat salmon, lake trout, brown bullheads, catfish, smallmouth bass or eels. State plans to construct a new $10 million salmon and trout hatchery generated considerable controversy when it became clear that the fish would become contaminated upon release.[7] Similar findings of fish contamination, as well as controversy over increased fish plantings, occurred in Michigan where fishermen were advised not to eat salmon more than once a week. The director of the Department of Natural Resources decided not to expand the salmon program as had been proposed.

2. On January 14, 1977, the National Sea Clammers Association filed a $250 million class-action suit in federal court on behalf of clammers, lobstermen and fishermen charging that various officials of New York City, New York State, the state of New Jersey, the Army Corps of Engineers and the Environmental Protection Agency were negligent in allowing the pollution of a large area of Atlantic coastal waters which resulted in the loss of living resources.[8] The suit was based upon occurrences during the summer and fall of 1976 off the north shore

of New Jersey, where there were two major fish kills, causing mortality rates as high as 50%. An algae bloom and anoxic (oxygen depletion) conditions destroyed an estimated $14-16 million worth of finfish stocks and up to $22.5 million of shellfish.[9] Of particular concern was the possibility that the $50 million surf clam industry may have received long-range damage since one of the major kills took place during July, which is the normal spawning season for surf clams. It is not clear what contribution sewage sludge disposal had upon these kills. However, the evidence is compelling that this important section of Atlantic coastal waters is increasingly unable to sustain finfish or shellfish.

3. On November 16, 1976, a class-action suit representing some 10,000 persons including crabbers, clammers, shell fishermen, oyster tongers, seafood wholesalers, boat and restaurant owners was filed against the Allied Chemical Corporation for some $8.8 billion in damages resulting from the contamination in 1975 of the James River with Kepone by a plant under contract to Allied.[10]

4. Studies of oysters, clams and mussels in coastal waters of Washington, Oregon, Virginia, Delaware, Maryland, Connecticut, Rhode Island, Massachusetts and Maine revealed the presence of significant numbers of neoplasms (tumors). While these tumors may not preclude human consumption, they may indicate a rise in coastal water pollution. One of the researchers involved in the studies observed that while a decade ago only a few cases of unusual growth in shellfish were reported, in recent years they have been counted in large numbers.[11]

5. In January of 1977, the New York State Department of Environmental Conservation began to advise residents on the north shore of Long Island not to eat striped bass or large bluefish more than once a week, due to elevated PCB levels. It was emphasized that residents who had just one meal a week of bluefish or bass were "perfectly safe."[12]

6. On December 18, 1976, a coalition of fishermen filed a $60 million class-action suit against the Thebes Shipping Company, owners of the oil tanker *Argo Merchant*. Earlier that week this tanker broke in two on a Nantucket shoal and in the worst

oil spill in the nation's history[13] spilled some 7 million gallons of Number 6 "Bunker C" fuel oil into the Atlantic Ocean.

A further threat to fisheries management is the continued destruction of specific habitat areas such as reefs and estuaries, both of which are vital for feeding or breeding grounds. Dredging and filling has led to the loss of an estimated 4% of the nation's coastal habitat areas between 1950 and 1969.[14] As the need for dredge spoil disposal sites continues or increases, combined with a growing interest in the extraction of offshore deposits of sand and gravel, it is expected that coastal water habitats will become further endangered.

In attempting to integrate a comprehensive living resource management program into their coastal waters planning efforts, the states face a difficult task. Perhaps the greatest difficulty involved is that demand for the use of coastal waters for a wide variety of human activities is expected to intensify. These water uses have and will impart changes (both physical and chemical) upon the coastal water environment. Yet most finfish and shellfish have a limited ability to survive such changes. Their survival is primarily dependent upon genetically based biological limitations which are not always amenable to human multiple-use management schemes based upon other criteria.

CASE HISTORIES

There are several recent examples of fisheries disputes or problems that collectively reflect the scope of the coastal water management task. It is a task that involves not only complex natural systems, but also difficult problems of human conflict.

Jeffreys Ledge, Maine

Jeffreys Ledge is a fertile fishing ground off the coast of southern Maine which is frequented by both gill-netters and draggermen. Disputes have arisen between the two types of fishing, since on occasion gill nets have been damaged or destroyed by the draggers. This situation has been complicated by the fact that gill-netters fishing Jeffreys Ledge tend to reside in Maine, and draggermen fish out of Gloucester, Massachusetts.

The conflicts developed to the point where the situation was referred to by some as "the Battle of Jeffreys Ledge."

Resolution: At least for the present this conflict appears to have been reduced, if not resolved. The two groups of fishermen have met, along with observers from various state, regional and federal agencies, to discuss a fisheries management plan for the Jeffreys Ledge area. The plan, primarily an informal set of agreements between the two groups, includes the use of mutual radio channels, the preparation and distribution of charts showing where gill nets are deployed, and the establishment of a formal mediation arrangement.[15]

Savannah River Shrimp Grounds

The border between the states of Sourth Carolina and Georgia includes the Savannah River system, as defined by the Treaty of Beaufort in the 18th century. Because the actual location of the Savannah River has fluctuated over time, both Georgia and South Carolina claim jurisdiction over a 300-square-mile ocean area.

To a considerable extent, the issue is not that of shrimp harvesting but of jurisdiction. Specifically, the issue concerns which state has the authority to control fishing in a particular coastal water area. South Carolina allows shrimping to start in late May, while Georgia does not open its season until June. If the coastal waters in question are under Georgia's jurisdiction, the South Carolina shrimpers are violating Georgia law and their boats may be confiscated. If South Carolina controls the area, then Georgia's management plan is voided by the early fishing allowed under South Carolina regulations.

Resolution: This type of dispute tends to have long historic roots, and may take some time to resolve. However, it should serve as a signal to some states to give detailed consideration to the establishment of precise descriptions of its coastal water boundaries, including not only those between it and other states, but also at the state-federal interface at the three-mile limit. In some instances, state boundaries other than the landward ones are somewhat imprecise for their coastal zone. With increased use, conflicts and opportunities, the question of which set of regulations will apply may be critical, and as some states have already learned, a matter of feet and inches can have significant and long-range implications. The advantages of establishing precise boundaries, taking whatever actions are necessary prior to expanded development, cannot be overemphasized.[16]

California Anchovy Fishery

The California Anchovy Fishery is under considerable fishing pressure. The anchovy is used by sport fishermen for gamefish bait and is taken by commercial seiners for sale to reduction plants where the fish are converted into fish oils, fertilizers and protein for chicken feed. California fishermen, both commercial seiners and sports fishermen, compete with commercial boats out of Mexican waters. A new $15 million reduction plant and fishing fleet in Ensenada, Mexico, is expected to further increase this pressure.

The California Fish and Game Commission supported by the California Department of Fish and Game, regulates this fishery. In 1976, their regulations included the designation of a fishing season, which was August 1-May 15 for a northern area and September 15-May 15 for the southern management area. Quotas were set at 100,000 tons of anchovies for the southern management area and 15,000 tons for the northern management area.

The issues facing the California Fish and Game Commission involve determining how much harvesting the anchovy fishery can support on a sustained yield basis and how the allowable catch should be allocated between the two interest groups. Commercial seiners desire larger quotas, claiming that if California commercial seiners do not harvest the fish, they will be caught by Mexican fishermen, since the fishery extends beyond California's coastal waters. Sports fishermen claim that anchovies are a critical bait species, and that necessary forage for game fish populations will be depleted if commercial seining continues. They further claim that the current reduction in anchovy stocks is a result of excessive commercial harvesting.

Resolution: Until such time as marine biologiest can establish the cause of anchovy stock decline, and of sustainable yields, the merits of either claim are unclear. The Fishery Conservation and Management Act of 1976 calls for the protection and improvement of both commercial and recreational fishing. Yet these two fishing interests may not always be compatible, just as various forms of commercial fishing may conflict. Through a formal coastal zone management mechanism, more interactions between land and water uses and between different coastal water activities can be accommodated within a given time and space. Yet the biological carrying capacity of a particular coastal water system may be relatively fixed and is, in many instances, being diminished by the introduction of pollutants. In some instances, expanded or protected fisheries may only be possible if other activities are excluded from coastal waters, or if the fisheries are managed so as to serve a primary user group, rather than attempting to provide multiple use.

Virginia Menhaden Fishery

The state of Virginia has established regulations over fishing activities in its half of Chesapeake Bay which include provisions that prohibit non-U.S. citizens from fishing within the three-mile limit of coastal waters and, of equal importance, also prohibits nonresident commercial fishermen from its coastal waters.

As described in Chapter 2, the Submerged Lands Act appears to give full title over submerged lands and "natural resources within such lands and waters" within the territorial sea to the states. However, as the discussion of basic federal authority attempted to convey, there are several federal powers, such as those for interstate commerce, that can preempt or constrain a state action even under the authority granted by the Constitution, the courts or Congress.

Seacoast Products, Inc. of Port Monmouth, New Jersey, has taken the state of Virginia to court over the regulations, attempting to have them overturned. A three-judge federal court decided that the regulation of aliens was a power reserved to the federal government by the Constitution, and that the laws are unconstitutional.

Resolution: The case arose from competition over menhaden stocks in the Atlantic Ocean and Chesapeake Bay. Several states have fishing residency laws as one method of regulating access to coastal fisheries. These are being challenged as nonresidents attempt to use finite coastal resources. A connected issue is that of beach access. Many communities prohibit nonresident use of certain coastal beaches or charge a special fee not applied to residents.

Because of the importance of this case to the authority of states to regulate their coastal fisheries, Virginia was supported by Maine, Maryland, Massachusetts, New York and Delaware in asking the U.S. Supreme Court to review the case. On May 23, 1977, the Supreme Court ruled that the Virginia laws are invalid insofar as they exclude nonresidents. The extent to which this decision will limit future state efforts at regulation of coastal fisheries is not yet clear. However, it emphasizes the complexities of coastal waters management and the degree to which a variety of federal laws and policies must be considered in any state management effort.

THE PROBLEMS OF MANAGEMENT

There are several problems of fisheries management that will affect most coastal water management programs.

Shore Facilities

In many coastal areas, industrial and residential development has either precluded or begun to conflict with commercial and recreational fishing activities. If the objectives of the Fishery Conservation Act and other federal programs are met, there will be a significant growth in domestic commercial fishing, as well as in aquaculture and recreational fishing. There will be a need for more boat and fish processing facilities; yet these facilities must compete economically, aesthetically and politically with a growing list of other activities that also use shore and water resources. In many communities, traditional patterns of land use are changing, and new zoning may preclude storage of equipment or other activities associated with commercial fishing. New OCS developments will require shore support facilities, including harbor space for service vessels, and these new interests may displace commercial fishing. If market economics becomes the sole method of coastal access allocation, commercial fishing could be in serious trouble.

Pollution from Fish Processing

The Environmental Protection Agency has estimated that 38% of all fish processing plants will have to be exempted from federal water quality requirements if they are to remain open, and that even with such exemptions, 16% will be forced to close. In the fall of 1976, seven sardine plants were fined by the Maine Department of Environmental Protection when they failed to meet an October 1 deadline for the installation and proper operation of water pollution control equipment.[17] As activities such as shore-based recreation and coastal residential development expand, several traditional water-based activities such as fishing and fish processing will require additional attention if they are not to be displaced by competing uses and more stringent standards. Special shore and water areas may have to be set aside for commercial fishing and related facilities. Otherwise they may not be compatible with other coastal uses, due to smell or other activity characteristics. The idea of special seafood processing parks, such as that now being considered for the Beaufort, South Carolina, area[18] may be of increasing importance.

As discussed in Chapter 1, coastal waters present some different management problems (and opportunities) than coastal lands. Fisheries management represents a prime example of this. Due to the nature of the water environment, the entire territorial sea, as well as any activity that affects them, is of concern to fisheries management. It is difficult, if not impossible, to isolate activities and their impacts to the degree that can be done on land. This may necessitate greater use of management devices such as exclusive-use zones, and may ultimately require some exclusion of types or amounts of activities from entire coastal water regimes to properly protect and enhance priority water uses.

Chlorine

Chlorine is used to "treat" human sewage, and to clean heat exchangers in power plants. More than 5000 tons of this chemical are released into coastal and inland waters each year.[19]

Federal standards tend to encourage heavy use of chlorine in sewage treatment, and some communities add extra amounts to provide a residue of "free" chlorine for added protection. Virginia, for example, requires that its effluent must have 2 ppm of free chlorine to protect its shellfish industry from contamination by viruses such as polio and hepatitis.[20]

However, both shellfish and finfish are very sensitive to chlorine. Oyster larvae, supposedly protected by extra amounts of free chlorine, die when exposed to chlorine levels nearly a thousand times lower than 2 ppm.[20] In terms of finfish and shellfish management, chlorine can be seen as a toxic pollutant. But the problem is even more complicated. In some instances chlorine reacts with the organic compounds in sewage, forming chlorinated hydrocarbons that may be as dangerous as PCBs. It has also been discovered that once discharged into coastal waters, chlorine can be displaced by bromine, thus forming brominated hydrocarbons related to chemicals such as PBB. As one research scientist has said: "That's good, hard evidence that we don't know what we're doing."[21] If present techniques of secondary treatment of sewage continue, and if flush water from power plants continues to be discharged into coastal and estuarine waters, large areas of coastal waters could be rendered unfit for living resources.

Conflicts Among Fishing Groups

Marine recreational fishing, which includes the harvesting of shellfish as well as finfish for personal use, has become a major coastal water use activity in the United States. Recent surveys estimate that there are almost 30 million marine recreational fishermen, and this number may increase by as much as an additional 15 million by 1985.[22] This creates an expanded demand for shore access and water surface use. It also represents a growing potential for conflict between recreational and commercial harvesting of finite fishery stocks. This type of conflict is further complicated by regional disagreements between different commercial fishing interests, including several important instances in which the courts have upheld historic fishing rights for native Americans. In some instances these decisions have led to a court-ordered management system which excluded other U.S. citizens from fishing grounds during part or all of the fishing season.

Perhaps the best-known treaty rights case led to a decision in February of 1974 by U.S. District Court Judge George Boldt. In that decision Judge Boldt determined that due to historic fishing rights certain treaty Indians must be allowed to take or attempt to take 50% of all harvestable salmon in the state of Washington's salmon runs.[15] Since then there has been a growing number of clashes between fishermen and enforcement officers, including the shooting of one fisherman. Recently similar fishing rights were recognized in Michigan's Upper Peninsula.

As described earlier, there has been increasing conflict between commercial anchovy seiners and sport fishermen in California, the problem being that there may not be enough anchovies for both interest groups. In Michigan, a similar concern has led to the prohibition of the use of gill nets by commercial fishermen and the creation of water zones to protect certain stocks for recreational fishing.

At the present time, American commercial fishing represents a $1 billion industry, employing some 500,000 people directly or indirectly. Additionally, some 30 billion people enjoy marine fishing (including shellfish harvesting) as a recreational activity:

> "Our fisheries are one of the nation's—indeed the world's— greatest resources, and will become increasingly important as a source of food for man in the decades ahead. We cannot permit the depletion of our fishstocks and the destruction of fish habitats to continue. We must learn to manage this re- source so that we may use it to the optimum now and so that future generations may be able to use it and draw even greater yields from it. _And we can and must do it in ways which are compatible with the nation's need to develop other valuable uses of the ocean._"[23] (emphasis added)

Translating these objectives into a workable state coastal man- agement program will obviously be difficult. It may soon be necessary for both state and federal management programs to determine how much of finite fish stocks should be used by which groups. To make such choices, new decision rules may have to be invented by the public. Such decisions have been avoided by increasing access facilties or putting more money into fisheries management. These choices are difficult not only technically, but also politically.

Direct Conflict with Other Coastal Users

As more people attempt to use the coastal zone for an expanding number of activities, conflicts will increase in number and severity. As reflected in recent court actions cited earlier, people engaged in various aspects of the fishing industry are now attempting to influence shore- and water-use decisions so as to protect their perceived interests in clean waters, sufficient harbor and processing sites, and protection of nearshore and deepwater habitats. Since finfish and shellfish are extremely sensitive to habitat loss and changes in coastal water characteristics, virtually every coastal water use proposal is likely to be viewed by those in the fishing industry or recreational fishermen as a potential threat to their interests. If aquaculture, recreational fishing and commercial fisheries are improved and expanded, as intended by the passage of the Fishery Conservation Act of 1976, there will then be an increased need for careful siting of facilities; for water and shore zones to protect habitat and fish harvesting areas; and for frequent evaluation of the type and amount of activity that can occur with coastal waters in harmony with expanded fisheries. For example, the February 1977 issue of *National Fisherman* reports the strong opposition of Virginia oyster packers to a proposed 250,000 bbl/day oil refinery that would be constructed in Portsmouth, Virginia, and discharge into the Elizabeth River. The number of interest groups wishing to participate in a coastal management decision is likely to grow as coastal management plans are implemented, making allocative choices increasingly difficult and complex.

THE FISHERY CONSERVATION ACT OF 1976

In 1976, the United States established a 200-mile economic zone adjacent to its territorial waters. The basic intent of the Fishery Conservation Act, by which this zone was established, is to insure that commercial fish harvesting is limited to rates that the resource can support over time, and the American fishermen be given priority access to fisheries' resources along our coasts. It also establishes a mechanism for a new level of comprehensive fisheries management.

Aside from the 200-mile zone, in which foreign vessels can fish only with a federal permit, the major features of this Act are eight Regional Fishery Management Councils which the Act authorizes:

1. *New England Fishery Management Council:* consists of 17 voting members and includes the states of Maine, New Hampshire, Massachusetts, Rhode Island and Connecticut and has authority over the fisheries in the Atlantic Ocean seaward of those states.
2. *Mid-Atlantic Fishery Management Council:* consists of 19 voting members and includes the states of New York, New Jersey, Delaware, Pennsylvania, Maryland and Virginia, and has authority over the fisheries in the Atlantic Ocean seaward of those states.
3. *The South Atlantic Fishery Management Council:* consists of 13 voting members including the states of North Carolina, South Carolina, Georgia and Florida and has authority over the fisheries in the Atlantic Ocean seaward of those states.
4. *The Caribbean Fishery Management Council:* consists of 7 voting members including the Virgin Islands and the Commonwealth of Puerto Rico and has authority over the fisheries in the Caribbean Sea and Atlantic Ocean seaward of those stated.
5. *The Gulf of Mexico Fishery Management Council:* consists of 17 voting members including the states of Texas, Louisiana, Mississippi, Alabama and Florida, and has authority over the fisheries in the Gulf of Mexico seaward of those states.
6. *The Pacific Fishery Management Council:* consists of 13 voting members, including the states of California, Oregon, Washington and Idaho and has authority over the fisheries in the Pacific Ocean seaward of those states.
7. *The North Pacific Fishery Management Council:* consists of 11 voting members and includes the states of Alaska, Washington and Oregon and has authority over the fisheries in the Arctic Ocean, Bering Sea and Pacific Ocean seaward of Alaska.
8. *The Western Pacific Fishery Management Council:* consists of 11 voting members, and includes the state of Hawaii,

American Samoa and Guam, and has authority over the
fisheries in the Pacific Ocean seaward of such states.

These councils have authority to formulate management plans
that will directly affect the fisheries of coastal states. New
fishing patterns and domestic pressures, increased promotion of
aquaculture and economic shifts may result from council actions.

STATE COASTAL MANAGEMENT PROGRAMS
AND THE FISHERY COUNCILS

The Fishery Conservation Act contains several safeguards to
insure that state authority to manage coastal fisheries is not
diminished. The governors of the affected states appoint most
of the members of the councils, and the state director of
fisheries management is included as a voting member on the
council. Furthermore, state plans can be adopted by the council
and Section 306 specifies that state jurisdiction over coastal
waters is not to be extended or diminished by the Act.

However, there is some basis for concern. Section 306(b)
stipulates that the Secretary of Commerce can, under certain
conditions, assume management responsibilities of a specific fishery within the boundaries of a state if and as long as a state's
management program fails to meet the Secretary's approval.

Also of concern is the possibility that these new regional
councils, in formulating regional fisheries management plans, will
interfere with state coastal zone management efforts. Council
plans for increased fisheries development could conflict with
state coastal water management objectives of industrial development, or may generate shore access pressures inconsistent with
a state plan. While the state is given a strong role in council
activities, there is no assurance that these activities will be
coordinated with coastal management efforts. In some instances
fisheries management is a separate state function, and communication may not occur unless the state coastal management
program sends an observer to council meetings and makes other
efforts to clarify the process and goals of the coastal management program. Otherwise, state coastal managers might have
to evoke the consistency clauses of the CZMA.

There are several positive aspects to the Fishery Conservation Act. For the first time, the state coastal management programs (CZMP) can interact with a cohesive federal ocean fishery management system. These regional councils have the potential to increase the ability of states to manage finfish and shellfish within coastal waters. Inventory and habitat protection efforts by the councils can augment state efforts, especially if they are coordinated. Regional fisheries management plans can join with state programs to privde a systems approach to each fishery, going beyond the limits of the territorial sea. With a proper interface between coastal management and the regional councils, provision of shore facilities, habitat protection and coordination with other types of coastal water activity can be achieved.

MANAGEMENT APPROACHES

Even with regional councils, coastal states face a number of fisheries management problems, including marine pollution, insufficient shore facilities and a limited fish population. Most states are now trying one or more techniques to keep fishing pressure within the limits of fish stock. Some of these techniques include:

1. *closed seasons or areas* in which fishing is prohibited when or where the stocks are most vulnerable. These are spatial or temporal exclusion zones;
2. *limits on size* of certain species, to insure that species reach a size or age where they can reproduce;
3. *vessel limitations*, such as size, tonnage, or automotive power restrictions, designed to reduce pressure on the stocks by imposing technological inefficiency;
4. *limited entry*, in which only a certain number of fishermen or a certain number of boats are allowed to harvest a particular species. Sometimes vessels are purchased from the state, both as compensation and to insure limited fishing pressure;
5. *gear restrictions* designed for the same purpose as vessel limitations, or to make harvesting more selective, for either a specific species or a certain age class; and
6. *limits on catch*, which result in closing a fishery once the total allowable catch has been reached.

The Coastal Zone Management Act allows states to augment such approaches with a comprehensive regulation of activities to insure that critical habitat, necessary shore facilities and required water quality continue to exist. By designating areas of particular concern, priorities of use, and permissible and nonpermissible uses in shore and water areas, the state coastal program can not only assure continued commercial and recreational fisheries, but also place them within the broader context of multiple resource use, balancing fisheries needs against other activities and other resource parameters.

A traditional state fishery program could not really hope to regulate water quality, surface water use, dredge spoil disposal, ocean dumping, estuarine fill and all the other factors that can endanger a continued fishery. But if living resources are to be protected and improved as part of a state CZMP, there are certain implications for program design that must be considered. Finfish and shellfish are highly reactive to most changes in the marine environment, especially thermal and chemical changes. They are interlinked in extraordinarily complex and sensitive biogeochemical webs that must be maintained. In many instances the concept of multiple use is difficult if not impossible to translate into allocative patterns compatible with fisheries management. In some instances a choice between a viable fishery or another set of uses may be required. Both may not be possible in the same environment. Spatial separation, which can work quite effectively in land use management, has less impact in coastal waters, where there is constant interchange through the aquatic medium. Since the demand for coastal water access for purposes other than fishing can be expected to grow, great care must be given to identifying conditions under which activities might be compatible, and priorities constantly reassessed.

OREGON

On January 1, 1977, a new set of statewide planning and management goals and guidelines went into effect for the state of Oregon. Adopted by the Land Conservation and Development Commission, these goals and guidelines indicate a clear understanding of the management needs of strong fisheries, and a choice to favor the management of living resources over other uses. This is a major choice, for from it flows the majority of priorities and permissible uses for the entire coastal zone. It is also a difficult choice, for Oregon, as well as all other coastal states, has a variety of needs beyond those of living resources management.

> *Goal 19: Ocean Resources*
>
> To conserve the long-term values, benefits, and natural resources of the nearshore ocean and the continental shelf.
>
> All local, state, and federal plans, policies, projects, and activities which affect the territorial sea shall be developed, managed, and conducted to maintain, and where appropriate, enhance and restore, the long-term benefits derived from the nearshore oceanic resources of Oregon.
>
> Since renewable ocean resources and uses, such as food production, water quality, navigation, recreation, and aesthetic enjoyment, will provide greater long-term benefits than will non-renewable resources, *such plans and activities shall give clear priority to the proper managment and protection of renewable resources.* (emphasis added)

CALIFORNIA COASTAL MANAGEMENT POLICY

The California Coastal Act (SB 1277) was established as law in 1976. It provides a strong policy statement regarding fisheries management and marine environmental protection.

> Section 30230:
>
> Marine resources shall be maintained, enhanced, and, where feasible, restored. Special protection shall be given to areas and species of special biological or economic significance. *Uses of the marine environment shall be carried out in a manner that will sustain the biological productivity of coastal waters and that will maintain healthy populations of all species of marine organisms adequate for long-term commercial, recreational, scientific, and education purposes.*

This policy statement, to the degree that it is adhered to and translated into coastal water allocative decisions, would have major impact upon all coastal water uses. In terms of management, it affords decision-makers a clear indication of how to choose among alternative patterns of coastal water use. It also provides a strong, relatively clear measure by which the state of California can evaluate pending federal activities under the consistency provisions of the Coastal Zone Management Act of 1972. It is, in effect, a performance standard that all coastal water uses must observe and meet if they are to be permitted.

> Section 30234:
>
> Facilities serving the commercial fishing and recreational boating industries shall be protected and, where feasible, upgraded. Existing commercial fishing and recreational boating harbor space shall not be reduced unless the demand for those facilities no longer exists or adequate substitute space has been provided. Proposed recreational boating facilities shall, where feasible, be designed and located in such a fashion as not to interfere with the needs of the commercial fishing industry.

To assure a strong commercial fishing industry, at least two major conditions must be protected and improved. First, the quality of the water environment must be maintained in a state that can support healthy populations of fish. Section 30230 declares that it is the policy of the state of California to manage coastal water uses on the basis of such maintenance.

But a second condition, which is becoming very serious in many coastal areas, is to provide adequate shoreside facilities. Fishing harbors were once thought of as picturesque settings by tourists and summer residents. But increasingly, the necessary docks, net storage areas, bait storage bins, fueling facilities and processing plants may be seen by some as nuisance activities that conflict with recreational and residential use of shore and water areas. Zoning at the local level may increasingly preclude activities necessary for successful commercial fishing operations.

Also, anchorage and dock space is becoming more difficult to obtain, as affluent recreational boaters and offshore oil workboats compete for limited water access facilities. Given the trends and forecasts for a continued growth in demand for shore and water access by a wide variety of activities, it would seem that deliberate enclaves must be set aside for commercial fishing activities, if they are to continue.

Clearly, the choice to favor fishing as a priority use has major impacts, and represents perhaps the single most important allocative decision that a coastal water use management program can make. If it is to be a priority use, then the negative impacts of all other water activities must be controlled on the basis of fishery management objectives. However, there can be few other coastal water uses that are more important; have more historic claim to adequate consideration; and that are as totally dependent upon the maintenance of a high-quality marine environment and adequate shore facilities. Given the pressures for expanded development of the waters and submerged lands of the marine environment, maintenance of adequate conditions for commercial and recreational fishing represents perhaps the greatest challenge to any state coastal management program.

REFERENCES

1. United States Department of Commerce. *A Marine Fisheries Program for the Nation* (July 1976), p. 14.
2. *Ibid.,* p. 15.
3. *Ibid.,* p. 9.
4. *Ibid.,* p. 6.
5. *Ibid.,* p. 5.
6. "Florida's Swordfish Bonanza Choked by FDA" *National Fisherman* (December 1976), p. 9-A.
7. Severo, R. *New York Times* (January 14, 1977).
8. Sullivan, J. *New York Times* (January 14, 1977).
9. *National Fisherman* (February, 1977).
10. *New York Times* (November 16, 1976).
11. Webster, B. *New York Times* (January 27, 1977).
12. Pett, A. *The Port Washington News* (January 20, 1977).
13. Robb, C. *The Cape Codder* (December 23, 1976).
14. U.S. Department of Commerce. *A Marine Fisheries Program for the Nation* (July 1976), p. 8.
15. *National Fisherman* (December 1976).
16. *Ibid.,* (November 1976).
17. *Ibid.,* (December 1976).
18. *Ibid.,* (March 1977).
19. Jolley, R. Oak Ridge National Laboratory, cited in Lawrence Wright, "Troubled Waters," *New Times* (May 13, 1977), p. 43.
20. Wright, L. "Troubled Waters," *New Times* (May 13, 1977), p. 43.
21. Carpenter, J. Department of Chemical Oceanography, University of Miami, cited in Lawrence Wright, "Troubled Waters," *New Times* (May 13, 1977), p. 43.

22. U.S. Department of Commerce. *A Marine Fisheries Program for the Nation* (July 1976), p. 9.
23. *Ibid.,* p. 3.

RECOMMENDED READINGS

General Accounting Office. *The U.S. Fishing Industry: Present Condition and Future of Marine Fisheries,* Vols 1, 2. Comptroller General of the United States (December 1976).

National Fisherman. A monthly newspaper covering fisheries management throughout the United States. Subscription information available from *National Fisherman,* 21 Elm Street, Camden, Maine 04843.

National Marine Fisheries Service and Fish and Wildlife Service. *Living Coastal Resources,* Office of Coastal Management (July 1976).

United States Congress, Committee on Commerce. National Ocean Policy Study. *Legislative History of the Fishery Conservation and Management Act.* U.S. Government Printing Office (1976).

United States Congress, Committee on Commerce. National Ocean Policy Study. *Congress and the Oceans: Marine Affairs in the 94th Congress.* U.S. Government Printing Office (1977), pp. 3-54.

United States Department of Commerce. *A Marine Fisheries Program for the Nation* (July 1976).

CHAPTER 6

NATIONAL DEFENSE

Principal Agencies: Department of Defense
                         National Aeronautics and Space Administration
Principal Legislation: Coastal Zone Management Act
                         Federal Aviation Act of 1958
                         Proclamation 2732 of 31 May, 1947
                         Military Public Lands Withdrawals Act

From the inception of proposed coastal management legislation, the Navy has expressed concern over what it has termed "potential encroachment" by state coastal authorities into matters of essential national security.[1] Considering that the Coastal Zone Management Act calls for state designation of "permissible land and *water* uses" and broad guidelines of "priority of uses in particular areas" (both in Section 305), the Navy's concern seems reasonable. Yet the language of the Coastal Zone Management Act provides a degree of protection for national security interests that is unequaled for any other federal interest, except, to a lesser extent, for the Clean Air and FWPCA concerns of EPA.

NATIONAL DEFENSE REQUIREMENTS OF THE CZMA

National security is assured extraordinary consideration in the development and implementation of state coastal programs through two types of provision of the Coastal Zone Management Act. First, there is a set of general provisions that requires the

105

incorporation of all appropriate federal interests in state programs.

> Section 306(c) (1) requires that prior to approval of a state program, the state must demonstrate that it has provided an opportunity to all relevant federal agencies for *full participation* in program development.
>
> Section 306(c) (8) requires that the state management program provide for:
> > "...adequate consideration of the national interest involved in the siting of facilities necessary to meet requirements which are other than local in nature."
>
> Section 307(b) requires that each state demonstrate that the views of federal agencies principally affected by such programs have been adequately considered.

Sections 923.15, 923.31 and 923.32 of OCZM's regulations on 306 program approval support these requirements. However, in terms of national security, the Act goes much further.

> Section 307(c) (3) (A). Section 307 is the basic consistency clause of the CZMA. Section 307(c) (3) (A) stipulates that a license or permit can be granted by a federal agency even when it is inconsistent with a state's program if the Secretary of Commerce finds that the activity is *"necessary in the interest of national security."*
>
> Section 307(c) (3) (B) related to OCS development activities, and was added to the CZMA in 1976 amendments. It also allows for a federal override of state objections to a proposed inconsistent action if the Secretary of Interior finds that the proposed action is *"necessary in the interest of national security."*
>
> Section 307(d) requires that any federal assistance to state or local governments must be consistent with a state's CZMP. However, this section again contains an override provision, allowing a determination by the Secretary of Commerce that the proposed assistance is *"necessary in the interest of national security."*

POTENTIAL CONFLICTS

Some states are not accustomed to systematically dealing with a multitude of federal agencies as part of their state management process. As the 1976 GAO report on the CZMA suggests, several states had initial difficulty in developing a working relationship with federal agencies. Also, many federal agencies such as the Navy are not accustomed to frequent consultations with state management people as part of their management and permit process. The Coastal Zone Management Act, especially as it relates to coastal water use management, represents a unique challenge to both groups.

One possible problem would be a conflict over what constituted *"the national security."* It is conceivable that a federal agency might evoke national security to avoid state regulations or consistency review. While there is a strong presumption of federal supremacy in such matters, it will be increasingly difficult for the Department of Defense (DOD) or other federal agencies to just declare "national security." The nature and priority of the national security issues involved may have to be demonstrated. An authority such as the Executive Office of the President or perhaps the federal courts may have to weigh the importance of the national security issue against the claims of a coastal state for the need to protect the integrity of its coastal management plan.

Since national security issues are often classified and may be inappropriate for widespread scrutiny, this represents a potential for very serious administrative and judicial problems.

NAVY POLICY REGARDING STATE AUTHORITY

Some conflicts between state and Navy interests have developed as states move towards 306 program approval. As part of its formulation of department interest in coastal air, land and water resources, the Navy has articulated a very strong position which deserves careful consideration.

> Regardless of the legislative jurisdictional status of the property involved, the United States may exercise in all places whatever jurisdiction is essential to the performance of its constitutional functions *without interference from any source.*
>
> Thus no state may exercise any authority which would in any way interfere with or restrict the United States in the use of its property or obstruct it in the exercise of any of the powers which the states have relinquished to the United States under

the Constitution. One of the powers expressly surrendered by the states under the Constitution is the power "to provide and maintain a Navy." *It follows that enforcement of a state law may not be permitted to interfere with any authorized naval function.*[2] (emphasis added)

CASE HISTORY:
STATE OF WASHINGTON CZMP DEVELOPMENT

The state of Washington contains many facilities and operational areas of particular interest to the Navy and other national security-related federal agencies. In March of 1975, the DOD was asked to comment upon Washington State's CZMP and OCZM's draft environmental impact statement for that plan.

In June of 1975, OCZM received a letter from the Deputy Assistant Secretary of Defense for Environmental Quality which stated rather simply that "we do strongly object to the final approval of the state plan at this time." The letter went on to explain:

> We object to the approval of the plan primarily because national security interests were not adequately considered in the program development.[3]

In more detailed comments upon the Washington plan, the Navy voiced several specific objections.

1. Navy land within the geographic boundary of the state's coastal zone had not been identified for exclusion from the zone.
2. The state plan gave no substantive discussion of intended policy regarding coastal waters or how such policy might affect the Navy.
3. The importance of Navy operations, as a necessary or priority use, was never recognized.
4. The Navy was not given adequate opportunity to participate in the formulation of the state program.

A full discussion of the Navy's concern and OCZM and state responses can be found on pages X-27 through X-58 of the final EIS for the state of Washington program.[3]

The General Accounting Office, in reviewing the Coastal Zone Management Act and its implementation, discussed the Washington

State situation. The GAO report concluded that federal participation in state programs had been a major problem for several states, and that the states, the federal agencies, and the Office of Coastal Zone Management should all improve their efforts in this area. As GAO observed:

> ". . . the Navy has interests in 32 separate geographical areas in Washington's coastal zone. These areas include installations, shipyards . . . mooring piers . . . combat maneuver and general operating areas, [and] gunnery ranges and testing areas. . . . Some prominent installations [include] the Trident Submarine Base, where $75 million of new construction is taking place. Further, the headquarters of the 13th Naval District is in Seattle. Yet Washington did not contact the Navy until after the state submitted its program to NOAA."[4]

Since that time several adjustments have been made in the Washington program. To a considerable extent, the concern of the Navy and of at least six other federal agencies that at first opposed approval of Washington's program was a procedural one, reflecting a lack of a full state-federal dialogue. However, as GAO and OCZM observed, this dialogue is a "two-way street." If federal agencies have coastal interests, then they have a responsibility to so notify the coastal states. And the states must realize that many federal programs are already "in place" within the coastal zone, or within adjacent land, air or water areas that would be affected by coastal zone policy.

NAVAL OPERATIONS IN COASTAL WATERS

To explain why the Navy is so concerned about its mission and about possible state interference with naval operations, this section provides a brief description of some of the Navy's activities. This discussion may also provide state managers with a degree of understanding of naval activities that may directly affect their state coastal waters, as well as possible areas of naval assistance in state program implementation.

The Navy, and above it, the Department of Defense, operate complex worldwide management systems. If they had the time, money and mandate, they could conceivably contribute many ideas on organization, administration and information systems that would be of considerable use to state coastal water use efforts. In general, the Navy is responsible for the training, testing and operation of aircraft, surface vessels and subsurface systems, often interacting in complex tactical networks. These are linked with each other through command systems that could be equated, on a large scale, with a state's central coastal management authority.

The concerns of the Navy are not restricted to the operation of its own complex global network of men, equipment and communications. It must also interact with all other uses of the air, water and subsurface environment, as well as land-use activities that may affect its mission. In each United States naval operation area, there is a functioning management system that tracks, evaluates and allocates use of the air above, the sea below and the surface of coastal waters.

Until recently, the Navy and the Department of Defense have been operating a de facto air, water, submerged lands and land use management system for purposes of national security. It is imperative that states use sensitivity and intelligence when attempting to interact with this important and complex system, one that has strong political and legal support. However, states are charged under the CZMA with developing a more comprehensive view of coastal use in which national defense is but one of several priorities.

NAVAL OPERATIONAL AREAS

The Navy has established various protective activity zones to facilitate its operations. Coastal states may find these zones of particular interest as possible models for state management approaches to coastal water use management. These zones are often temporal in nature, which specific hours applied to them. During these periods, special activities take place within the zone and special restrictions upon public use are imposed. There are also complex *spatial* zones, that may include a particular section of air, surface waters, the water column, submerged lands or some combination of these.

1. *National or Regional Operational Systems:* The Navy and other federal agencies maintain a series of national security-

related systems on a national or coastwide basis, which include coastal waters. Special Air Defense Identification zones, radar monitoring areas, communications systems and electronic systems are included in these zones.

2. *Specific Operational Areas:* The Navy uses a series of activity zones to support its activities, many of which are located within coastal waters.

(a) *Special Use Airspace:* This may include prohibited, restricted, warning, alert, controlled firing and air traffic control air zones. They are identified on all coastal charts, and are established through requests to the Federal Aviation Administration. FAA approval is granted under authority of the *Federal Aviation Act of 1958* and *Executive Order 10854 of 1959.*

These air space areas may include surface waters, when they are over the territorial waters, but do not affect state-controlled submerged lands. Airspace areas over international waters always include the underlying waters, but not submerged lands of the continental shelf.

The principal coastal area use of such airspace designations is to allow the use of aircraft, air-based weapon systems, ground to air systems, and the use of land-based weapons or sea-based weapons that may transit through an air corridor. Without special reservation of this pace, non-military aircraft and other activities might be endangered, or disrupt military activities.

(b) *Anchorages and Restricted Water Areas:* These may include:

caution areas, controlled firing areas, danger areas, fleet operating areas (FLT OPAREA), warning areas, prohibited areas, restricted areas, special use areas and security areas. The Navy also operates submarine transit lanes, explosive and chemical dumping areas and sea defense areas.

These areas are under the control of a designated scheduling authority within the district commandant administration. They are marked on charts, and are established under federal law using the authority of Proclamation 2732 of 31 May, 1947, (see Chapter 3) and are designated by the Department of the Army, Corps of Engineers.

An Example:
Naval Surface Weapons Center, Solomons Facility[4]

The Naval Surface Weapons Center (NAVSURFWPNCEN) is a 296-acre site at Point Patience, Calvert County, Maryland, on the Patuxent River, Chesapeake Bay.

In 1941 under the Bureau of Ships, this site was developed as the Naval Mine Warfare Test Station to undertake research and development work on mine warfare and counter measures. The use of the site then went through a series of changes, until September of 1974 when it became the Naval Surface Weapons Center.

Its mission is to conduct air, surface and underwater field trials on full-scale samples of ordnance in the Patuxent River or Chesapeake Bay. In addition, a Naval Recreation Center and a hydrographic research project of the Naval Oceanographic Office are located within the facility.

Unique Site Characteristics

Water depths of 150 feet in the Chesapeake Bay and 130 feet in the Patuxent River are important for the testing of marine equipment and are unique for Eastern and Gulf inland and coastal waters. It is therefore questionable that similar facilities could be obtained at some other regional coastal facility. Also, the sheltered nature of these waters facilitates shock testing of new ordnance components. The river range, which is adjacent to the facility, has both depth and bottom characteristics which facilitate testing and recovery of test units.

Because of deep water, large naval vessels can be brought to NAVSURFWPNCEN for electromagnetic pulse radiation (EMP) impact testing, using a special EMPRESS (Electromagnetic Pulse Radiation Environment Simulator for Ships) system. The Navy feels that the characteristics of this site justify setting it aside for Naval use.

Ranges

There are several ordnance test areas, including land, air, surface and subsurface use:

1. *Patuxent River Range:* includes three sites for testing ordnance air dropped into water environments such as mines, bombs, antisubmarine warfare weapons, and sonobuoys. This is a water zone about 0.5 nautical miles wide and 4 nautical miles long.
2. *Chesapeake Bay:* possible uses include wide areas of the bay, which is some 80 nautical miles long and an average of 7 nautical miles wide. A deepwater test site of 146 acres exists near the mouth of the Patuxent River.
3. *Bloodsworth Island:* located 25 miles from the Solomons facility, this island and surrounding waters are used for the testing of shallow water ordnance and firing of gun rounds up to 152 mm in size.

Other test areas are included on the land portions of the site.

Water Security

In effect, the Navy has established several water zones for weapons and systems testing. To insure that the tests are not disrupted, and that the general public is not endangered, the Navy takes special actions to enforce these zones.

> *Public Listings:* as with all special air and water use areas, the Navy lists these areas on national ocean survey charts (NOAA), and in the *United States Coast Pilot 3* (Navigational Regulation 207.125).

As part of its coordination with state coastal zone management programs, the Navy has provided descriptions of such areas to each state. Typically, these zones are at some times restricted areas or time-managed water/air/subsurface zones. The Solomons Facility includes the following types of water use restriction areas, as described in Section 207.125 of Coast Pilot 3.

1. No person in the water and no craft shall approach closer than 75 yards to the beaches, shorelines, or piers of the area formerly occupied by the U.S. Naval Mine Warfare Test Station, or of U.S. Naval Air Station property.

> A person in the water or a civilian craft shall not approach rafts, barges, or platforms closer than 100 yards.

These restrictions represent a permanent buffer zone, insuring a 75-100 yard area separating the facility from other uses of Chesapeake Bay or the Patuxent River. Not only does this provide protection to the public, but also to facility users.

> 2. Seaplane landings and takeoffs will occasionally be practiced within a designated water zone on the Patuxent River, which is precisely described in the Coast Pilot and marked on area charts.
>
> When these zones are not being used, they are open to civilian water use.
>
> At those times when they are to be used for seaplanes, a series of indicators are used, and special restrictions enforced.

Consistency

In accordance with OCZM rules, all federal lands are to be excluded from designation as part of a state's coastal "zone." However, OCZM has also stated, in Washington State's EIS and elsewhere, that while certain facilities may be excluded, the impacts those facilities may impart upon coastal waters are still subject to review under the Section 307 consistency requirements of the Coastal Zone Management Act. Thus the Solomons Facility in Maryland would not be included within the boundary designation of Maryland's coastal zone, and consequently would not be subject to several of the CZMP provisions. But if the Solomons Facility was to have a direct or significant impact upon the coastal waters, to that degree it would have to interact with the state management program.

SOME NATIONAL ISSUES
IN DOD/STATE CONSISTENCY

As this chapter has described, Naval operations within United States coastal waters include the extensive use of air, submerged lands, water column and surface water zones. Sometimes these are reserved and operated as exclusive naval areas, even though they are within the coastal waters of the state.

The Coastal Zone Management Act specifically excludes certain lands, but does not exclude coastal waters.

> *Section 304(a)* . . . Excluded from the coastal zone are lands the use of which is by law subject solely to the discretion of or which is held in trust by the federal government, its officers or agents.

The United States Attorney General has ruled, and the Office of Coastal Zone Management has accepted, that this exclusion clause affects all federal lands. But again, what of coastal waters?

A careful reading of the Act and of the congressional hearings leading to its passage[2] would suggest that Congress did not give any indication of excluding water areas from state control. There is, in fact, some indication that this potential "problem" may not have received full consideration by Congress, and further clarification may be required.

Clearly, the Navy and other security-related agencies have an important mission that has been acknowledged by Congress through provisions of the CZMA and other legislation. Just as clearly, the Submerged Lands Act of 1953 recognizes state ownership and public trusteeship of the territorial zone.

The problem is twofold:

1. Unless the Coastal Zone Management Act is modified, the Navy and other federal agencies may be able to exclude coastal lands, but not equally important coastal waters directly adjacent to those coastal lands. The logic and benefit of excluding one but not the other is in some instances questionable.

2. Unless coastal states, rather than DOD, approve, mark and administer water zones, then conceptually and factually the state will have limited ability to affect comprehensive management of coastal waters.

STATE MANAGEMENT STRATEGY

It is hoped that many defense-related water use problems can be resolved by state-federal cooperation. But some basic issues may require resolution by the Office of Coastal Zone Management, Congress or the Executive Office of the President.

At the present time, coastal states are left with a somewhat unclear jurisdictional authority over surface water management.

There are major national DOD facilities which require a clear management status, rather than the present degree of growing uncertainty. Examples of these are the Eglin Air Force Base missile testing range in the Gulf of Mexico and the Pacific Missile Test Center range in the Santa Barbara Channel. In such instances new siting would be costly, both in terms of time and money, and replacement sites may be unavailable.[5]

Congress has indicated that the state may not be in a position to evaluate the actual necessity of a particular DOD facility or activity for purposes of national security. However, under the CZMA, the state has been designated as the focal point for coastal water use decisions. Clearly, DOD activities must come under state review and coordination to some degree. Otherwise, the state program could be no more than an accommodation of military interests.

It is suggested that as a first step, the state make an extra effort to fully understand, in great detail, just what national security-related facilities and/or activities are located in or intended for the state's coastal zone:

1. Why are they located at their present site?
2. What impacts do the uses and facilities have on the coastal environment and on other existent or potential uses?
3. Are these facilities or activities coastal-dependent? If so in what way(s)?
4. What is the national security-related nature of these activities and facilities?
5. Who is in charge of these operations, and what information can be obtained on a consistent, timely basis?

FUTURE PLANNING

Naval and other security-related activities are critical uses of the coastal zone. As with energy-related facilities, it is important to consider how and if such activities can be accommodated within a coastal zone. Also, such facilities and activities often have major impacts in terms of employment, housing, transportation and recreational patterns. These impacts, both positive and negative, should be considered in any evaluation of expansion plans for DOD activities. It is possible that important sites, such as those associated with the Eglin Air Force Base missile range, or the deepwater characteristics of the Cheasapeake Bay site used by the Solomons Facility, could be set aside for possible DOD use without any significant impact upon future coastal water use. It is also possible that other areas, such as sensitive breeding grounds or unique recreational areas, could be specifically designated as being inappropriate for security-related activities.

Security-related use of coastal resources deserves consideration as a designated priority use. Appropriate siting and performance criteria for such activities may also be considered by the state. When designating or revising areas of particular concern (APCs), consideration might be given to whether various security-related activities are appropriate for such APCs, and be specifically discussed within the state plan.

Since national security uses of coastal waters are important, another management approach that states may wish to consider would be to incorporate specific security-related activities, locations, or facilities as recognized and protected parts of the CZMP. They could be listed as priority uses, specified as permissible uses within certain areas, or provided with special management attention by designating them as areas of particular concern. Upon evaluation of DOD special air and water use areas, states may wish to include some of these areas specifically as APCs.

DOD ASSISTANCE

The Navy and other agencies concerned with national security have a considerable amount of information, experience and technical ability that may be of great assistance to state coastal management efforts. These resources are neither by mandate or design widely available for civilian or coastal management purposes. But it is possible that especially for areas of mutual state-federal concern, that special management assistance might be available. In most instances this would represent a new idea for both DOD and the states and would require a strong cooperative relationship.

DOD already provides public information and impact assistance for communities and states where DOD activities will impart major impacts. Somewhat similar in concept to the CEIP provisions of the DZMA, these programs may contribute considerable assistance to state programs.

NAVAL MANAGEMENT SYSTEMS

A field operation area such as the one in Southern California (SOCAL FLT OPAREA) involves high-density use of both air and water space over a wide expanse of sea and land. Extensive communications, radar, computers and a highly structured administrative system are necessary to avoid chaos. While few if any state coastal management programs presently have either the resources or the need for such a complex control mechanism, an evaluation of what has been done to establish coordination among air, surface and subsurface operations might have considerable value. It is perhaps in the areas of scheduling, administrative networks, and communication/information/computer systems that the Navy and other units within DOD could provide the greatest amount of assistance to coastal states when and if they find it necessary to construct more complex coastal management programs.

One method of plugging into these systems is through the FAA, the Coast Guard, and the Corps of Engineers, all of which tend to receive special notification of DOD activities. In addition there are some instances where these agencies must issue permits or regulations. Coastal managers might also attempt to receive information on a regular basis from the Navy such as that contained in NOTAM's (notice to airmen), NOTEMAR's (notices to mariners) and HYDROPACS (hydrographic information) issues by the Navy within the area of operation. Coastal managers should attempt to make direct contact with the naval scheduling officer or officers in charge of fleet operations within the coastal state.

CONCLUSIONS

Given the complex, extensive and sometimes sensitive nature of Navy activities as well as those of other national security-related federal agencies, it is possible that at some future point state coastal water use interests and those of the Navy or some other security-related agency will conflict. The resolution of each issue cannot be discussed without the facts of a specific case. However, there are some general factors to keep in mind.

1.   Congress has recognized national security as a priority use of coastal waters, and effort must be made to accommodate such activities.

2.   Comprehensive coastal zone management, and especially coastal water management, requires that more than security-related activities occur within state waters. If national security is a priority use, coastal states also have other federal, state, regional and local priorities that are as legitimate, and sometimes more pressing.

3.   The concept of coastal or water dependency, which several states are using as a criterion for priority designations and permissible use categories, can also be applied to national security activities.

4.   Some of the current authorities and authorizations under which national security activities take place deserve careful evaluation. Certain adjustments might be necessary or desirable.

5.   The best time to work out differences of policy or need is before final decisions are made. The Navy and other national security-related federal agencies may not always be willing to fully open their records and operations to state coastal managers, but they have given evidence of being willing to talk and to work with state programs.

6.   Realistically, some states can expect to be faced with proposed actions that they feel are clearly inconsistent with the state CZMP, yet which go to the Secretary of Commerce under a claim of "national security." While state programs cannot make final determination of the ultimate merits of such claims, they can make a full case for the importance of consistency with their program, documenting in detail the consequences of

failing to do so.   In some instances state-federal issues will
develop that will require congressional resolution, or mediation
by the Executive Office of the President.   At such points, the
state can at best expect to be a participant in the decisions,
for in fact these are issues of national interest.

7.   If the CZMA allows for override of state programs, it
also provides a mechanism for cooperation, and an opportunity
for participation in decisions which heretofore were often made
without any state input.

REFERENCES

1. Frosch, R., Assistant Secretary of the Navy.   Senate Committee on
   Commerce hearings, April 21, 1970.
2. Naval Facilities Engineering Command, Department of Defense.   *Naval
   District Washington Coastal Land Use Study,* Part One (July 1976).
3. Office of Coastal Zone Management.   *State of Washington Coastal
   Zone Management Program Final Environmental Impact Statement*
   (April 9, 1976), p. X-27.
4. General Accounting Office.   *The Coastal Zone Management Program:
   An Uncertain Future* (December 1976) Chapter 5.
5. Leary, R.   Office of Fleet Operations, U.S. Navy.   Also *Coastal Zone Management* (April 6, 1977), p. 5.

SOURCES

1. Commander Third Fleet OPAREA MANUAL (COMTHIRDFLTINST
   3120.1H) June 11, 1973.
2. "Naval District Washington Coastal Land Use Study," Cheasapeake
   Division, Naval Facilities Engineering Command (July 1976).
3. Office of Fleet Operations, Cpt. R. Leary.
4. Office of Naval Oceanographer, Lt. Cmd. Yesky.
5. OPNAV Instruction 3100.5c "Navy Operating Area and Utilization of
   Coastal Shelf Program," (August 1974).
6. State of Washington Coastal Zone Management Program.   Final Environmental Impact Statement.

RECOMMENDED READING

Naval Facilities Engineering Command, Department of Defense.   *Naval
   District Washington Coastal Land Use Study,* Part One. (July 1976).

CHAPTER 7

DEEPWATER PORTS

Principal Agency: Department of Transportation
Principal Legislation: Deepwater Port Act of 1974

On December 17, 1976, Secretary of Transportation, William T. Coleman, approved the applications of LOOP, Inc. and SEA-DOCK, Inc. to construct deepwater ports off the coasts of Louisiana and Texas. Despite conditional approval, it is not yet clear that these deepwater ports will be constructed. However, the use of coastal or ocean waters for the construction and operation of deepwater ports is a coastal water use that deserves special consideration by all coastal states.

The continued import of foreign oil into U.S. coastal waters and future expansion of vessel transportation of materials will require major modification of the coastal environment.[1] The issue is not related strictly to the shipment of oil, although that has been the focus of most initial plans. The general problem facing most ports and waterways is lack of sufficient depth to accommodate a new generation of large ships, especially the 100,000-500,000 deadweight ton (DWT) supertankers. If coastal waters are to serve in part as a means for continued or increased economic development, there will be a growing demand for deeper and wider navigational channels. The impact of such modifications, which might include Great Lakes lock systems, harbors, ports, navigational channels and the construction of offshore facilities, could be significant. One strategy that has been increasingly advocated in the United States since the late 1960s has been the construction of some form of port facility in deep water, as an alternative to deepening the channels and harbors closer to shore.   Transfer of materials from this deepwater port to land would take place either through pipelines or by small coastal vessels that would not require major expansion of present channel depths.

While it is not clear what size tankers will be, due in large part to changing economics and the reopening of the Suez Canal, more than 55% of current world tanker capacity is in vessels of 100,000 DWT or larger.   A principal reason for the greater use of larger tankers in recent years is cost.   A 50,000 DWT tanker, of the type that typically serves such harbors as New York and Delaware Bay, averages 750 feet in length, 100 feet in width and 40 feet in draft.   A 250,000 DWT tanker is typically 1,100 feet long and draws 70 feet of water.   The key feature of the larger vessel is that it can carry five times as much oil at about half the price per barrel over long routes.[2] A saving that approaches 50% is a very strong stimulus both for private investment in the construction of such vessels and in consumer support for hopefully lower fuel costs.

A major problem with such vessels is that they are too large to operate in United States coastal waters.   With the exception of Puget Sound, no port on the west coast has a depth exceeding 55 feet.   The deepest port on the gulf coast is 40 feet, and there are not ports more than 45 feet deep on the east coast.   Long Beach and Los Angeles harbors in California and Puget Sound are the only three U.S. ports that can accommodate tankers of more than 100,000 DWT.[2]

Delaware Bay has a fairly typical delivery system.   More than two thirds of mid-Atlantic refinery capacity is in Delaware and New Jersey, and tankers must travel up the Delaware Bay and into the Delaware River to discharge their oil cargo.   The December 27, 1976, spillage of 134,000 gallons of oil by the tanker Olympic Games in the Delaware River illustrated the present and potential hazards of such a delivery system.   In many instances their delivery routes are in nearshore coastal waters where especially sensitive and important breeding grounds for finfish and shellfish exist, and where many shore-based coastal water activities take place.

Since the controlling depth of the Delaware River is 40 feet, large tankers now anchor inside Delaware Bay to pump their oil into barges or small tankers for final delivery to the refineries. This "lightering" process is commonly used in most coastal waters. In some instances the entire cargo is tranferred; at other times the cargo is partially transferred and the large tanker then is able to proceed, at reduced draft, into otherwise limiting navigation channels.

An example of what this might involve is given in the Office of Technology Assessment (OTA) Coastal Effects of Offshore Energy Systems report. The Japanese 191,000-DWT tanker *Yasutama Maru* arrived at the Big Stone Beach tanker anchorage in Delaware Bay on April 28, 1974. To lighter her cargo of 1,283,865 barrels of oil, it required 15 separate lightering operations, involving four trips of a 25,000-DWT tanker and 11 barge voyages to and from the Big Stone Beach anchorage. The reason for deepwater port support is reflected in a comment by the president of the Philadelphia Maritime Exchange who used the above example in testimony before the Delaware General Assembly. As he observed:

> "How much better and safer this could have been handled under the controlled conditions of a deepwater port which would permit a tanker to tie up to a platform, transferring its cargo into a pipeline, in a single operation, moving the oil via the pipeline direct to the refinery."[3]

For most coastal waters, a single-point mooring (SPM) system appears to be the most appropriate deepwater port facility. There are two basic types of SPM: the Catenary Anchor Leg Mooring (CALM) and the Single Anchor Leg Mooring (SALM), which OTA concluded in its analysis to be the safer of the two.[4]

To date, SPMs have had an impressive record of performance. More than 130 SPMs have been installed throughout the world since 1959.[5] The average oil spill rate at such terminals has been less than one barrel for every one million barrels handled, and it has been suggested that by using Very Large Crude Carriers (VLCC) in conjunction with deepwater ports that the number and volume of oil spills presently occurring with transhipment could be reduced by as much as a factor of ten.[5]

While deepwater ports of the SPM or other type appear to offer substantial reduction in oil spill hazard, especially where coastal waters are presently crowded, they have not been widely accepted by coastal states. By the early 1960s, considerable interest in the concept had emerged in the United States, and several projects were designed. The Corps of Engineers evaluated possible deepwater port sites in New York Bay, Delaware Bay, Cheasapeake Bay, the Mississippi River Delta, Freeport, Texas, Los Angeles/Long Beach area, San Francisco Bay and Puget Sound.[1]   The Deepwater Port Act of 1974 reflected a strong interest in this concept.

However, several states expressed partial or total opposition to such projects. In 1971, Delaware passed a Coastal Zone Act which specifically precludes the construction of any further heavy industry, including offshore unloading terminals. New Jersey has also expressed reservations concerning such projects. The construction of a deepwater port represents a major financial investment, and it is possible that such projects will not be constructed in less than a supportive political climate. Both the OTA study and the Department of Transportation LOOP Environmental Impact Statement conclude that there is little chance of a major deepwater port project being constructed within the eastern seaboard:

> "Over the past ten years, about 1.7 MBD of refining capacity proposed for the East coast has been rejected by local, regional, state or federal authorities or referenda; and 13 different proposals to construct deepwater port facilities have either been rejected or indefinitely postponed. Therefore, no deepwater port of a scale sufficient to divert significant quantities of crude oil from the Gulf Coast is anticipated or assumed for the U.S. East coast.[6]

However, as offshore development increases, coastal ports may become more crowded and potentially dangerous. And the full impacts of the energy shortages of the 1970s are not yet clear. It seems possible that conditions might at some point change sufficiently so as to stimulate further consideration of deepwater port construction in many coastal areas.

PRESENT REGULATORY SYSTEMS

Within State Waters

The Deepwater Port Act of 1974 applies only to waters outside the territorial sea, and does not affect deepwater ports that might be constructed within the more adjacent coastal waters. For such projects, within such coastal waters, the coastal state would have primary jurisdiction, which it might exercise quite effectively through a coastal zone management program. The state could justify such regulation through its ownership of submerged lands, its widely recognized police powers, the provisions of the Submerged Lands Act and the Coastal Zone Management Act of 1972.

The U.S. Army Corps of Engineers and the Coast Guard would also be involved in any coastal waters port project. Under authority of the Rivers and Harbors Act of 1899, the Corps has responsibility for insuring that such projects do not interfere with navigation. The Coast Guard, aside from mandates to facilitate navigation, would be specifically involved under the Ports and Waterways Safety Act. The federal Environmental Protection Agency and the Corps of Engineers might have further involvement, if such a project involved water disposal of dredge spoil.

To coordinate these diverse authorities, the coastal state could make creative use of its coastal management program, acting as a lead agency in processing the project proposal. In establishing such a control system, the coastal states might consider patterning their regulations after those of the Deepwater Port Act.

Beyond Coastal Waters

The Secretary of the Department of Transportation has been given the responsibility for coordinating deepwater port projects beyond the territorial sea under the provisions of the Deepwater Port Act of 1974. The first two proposals processed under the provisions of this Act (LOOP and SEADOCK) received conditional approval from the Secretary of Transportation in December, 1976.

The Act and the regulations that have been promulgated under its authority establish a comprehensive review process for each deepwater port project.[7]   This process may have a more general application for other types of activities proposed for coastal waters.

The Act and associated regulations establish a 45-day review process during which coastal states have an opportunity to comment upon the project.   Unless a coastal state already has a comprehensive coastal zone management program in place, and considerable information on coastal water resources, it may not be able to realistically respond within that time frame.

The license process includes two steps.   First a detailed application, including information specified in the rules and regulations, is prepared.   Then it is reviewed by states, federal agencies and interested members of the public.

THE ROLE OF THE STATE

The Deepwater Port Act and associated rules provide for state involvement at several points in this review process.

Section 4(d) requires that if a coastal state intends to construct a deep draft channel and harbor, that an offshore deepwater port license cannot be granted until the Secretary of Transportation evaluates the relative benefits of each alternative and also considers if the two are compatible or mutually exclusive.   Through this provision, the state gains assurance that a deepwater port beyond its jurisdiction will not be constructed in direct competition with a deep draft port proposed for coastal waters.

Section 5(g) requires that at least one public hearing on the project will be held in each adjacent coastal state.

Section 5(h)(1) requires that an applicant shall reimburse an adjacent coastal state for any costs incurred in processing an application.

Section 5(h)(2) allows adjacent coastal states to fix reasonable fees for the use of a deepwater port facility.   Any state in which land-based facilities directly related to a deepwater port facility are located may set reasonable fees for the use of such land-based facilities.

Section 5(i)(2)(A) requires that if more than one application for a particular area is submitted, then the license shall be issued to an adjacent coastal state or combination of states if they are among the competitors.

Section 4(c)(10) requires that the adjacent coastal state to which the deepwater port is to be directly connected by pipeline must have developed or be making reasonable progress toward developing an approved coastal zone management program.

Section 9(b)(1) is of critical importance. It stipulates that the Secretary of Transportation "shall not issue a license" without the approval of the governor of each adjacent coastal state. This section also allows the governor of an adjacent coastal state to identify aspects of the project which are inconsistent with its programs relating to environmental protection, land and water use, or coastal zone management. Under such circumstances, the Secretary can make the granting of a deepwater port license conditional upon alterations that will make the project consistent with such state programs.

DETERMINATION OF "ADJACENCY"

Section 9(b)(1) of the Deepwater Port Act gives the governor of "adjacent" coastal state veto power over a license application for a deepwater port project in federal waters. It also affords adjacent coastal states a special status which gives their suggestions and concerns a greater impact upon the decision process. It would be to the advantage of any state near a proposed deepwater port to achieve this designation.

Section 9(a)(1) of the Act specifies the criteria to be used for a designation of adjacency:

> The Secretary, in issuing notice of application pursuant to Section 5(c) of this Act, shall designate as an "adjacent coastal state" any coastal state which (a) would be directly connected by pipeline to a deepwater port as proposed in an application, or (b) would be located within 15 miles of any such proposed deepwater port.

Section 148.217 of the rules and regulations associated with the Deepwater Port Act provides a mechanism by which coastal states that have not been designated as adjacent coastal states can request such a designation. Such a request must make a claim that the proposed deepwater port represents a risk of damage to the coastal environment of the requesting state that is equal to or greater than the risk posed to a state directly connected by pipeline to the proposed port facility. In its evaluation of deepwater ports the Office of Technology Assessment observed that if a deepwater port was proposed for the east coast, the close proximity of several states would probably generate several formal requests for an adjacent coastal state designation from the Secretary of Transportation.[8]

Florida is the first state to have sought such a designation under the provisions of the Deepwater Port Act. Concerned about increased tanker traffic that would be generated by the SEADOCK and LOOP proposals, Florida claimed that increased vessel passages through the straits of Florida justified an adjacent state designation. The Department of Transportation disagreed. The Coast Guard and the Office of Coastal Zone Management developed conflicting conclusions as to the merits of Florida's claim, and Florida sought judicial relief. Eventually an accommodation was achieved, and the case dismissed. Florida secured a promise from the Secretary of Transportation that all of that state's concerns would be reflected in conditions imposed upon the licenses. It is difficult to determine whether Florida warranted adjacency designation under the intent and language of the Deepwater Port Act. But the adjacency provisions did allow a mechanism by which the state was recognized as having a legitimate interest in the federal licensing decision, even if the extent of that interest must, of necessity, be determined on a case by case basis.

REFERENCES

1. Institute for Water Resources. *U.S. Deepwater Port Study*, U.S. Army Corps of Engineers (August 1972), p. 5.
2. Office of Technology Assessment. *Coastal Effects of Offshore Energy Projects* (1976), p. 173.
3. *Ibid.*, p. 175.
4. Office of Technology Assessment. *Coastal Effects of Offshore Energy Projects* (1976), pp. 188-196.

5. Flory, J. "Oil Ports on the Continental Shelf," in *Oceanus.*
6. Department of Transportation. *Final Environmental Impact/4(f) Statement: Loop Deepwater Port License Application,* p. 5.
7. *Federal Register* (November 10, 1975).
8. Office of Technology Assessment. *Coastal Effects of Offshore Energy Projects* (1976), p. 195.

RECOMMENDED READINGS

1. *Deepwater Port Act of 1974* (Public Law 93-627) 33 U.S.C., pp. 1501-1525.
2. Department of Transportation. *The Secretary's Decision on the Deepwater Port License Application of LOOP, Inc.,* Washington, D.C. (December 17, 1976).
3. Department of Transportation. *The Secretary's Decision on the Deepwater Port License Application of SEADOCK, Inc.,* Washington, D.C. (December 17, 1976).
4. Institute for Water Resources. *U.S. Deepwater Port Study.* Department of the Army, Corps of Engineers (August 1972), volumes 1-5.
5. Office of Technology Assessment. *Coastal Effects of Offshore Energy Systems* (November 1976), volumes 1,2.
6. U.S. Coast Guard. "Deepwater Ports: Regulations on Licensing Regulations and Design Construction, Equipment and Operations Requirements; and Proposal on Site Evaluation." *Federal Register* (November 10, 1975).
7. U.S. Coast Guard. *Environmental Impact Statement: Deepwater Port Regulations (Final)* Deepwater Ports Project, Department of Transportation (1975).
8. U.S. Coast Guard. *Final Environmental Impact/4(f) Statement: LOOP Deepwater Port License Application,* Department of Transportation (1976).
9. U.S. Coast Guard. *Final Environmental Impact Statement: SEADOCK Deepwater Port License Application. Executive Summary. Department of Transportation* (1976).
10. U.S. Coast Guard. *Guide to Preparation of Environmental Analyses for Deepwater Ports,* Department of Transportation (1975).
11. U.S. Coast Guard. *Recommended Procedure for Developing Deepwater Ports Design Criteria,* Department of Transportation (1975).

CHAPTER 8

TANKER SAFETY

Principal Agency: U.S. Coast Guard (DOT)
Principal Legislation: Ports and Waterways Safety Act of 1972

The regulation of tanker traffic in coastal waters is as complex as any coastal water use management issue, and perhaps typifies better than most issues the potential disparity between a relatively narrow-focus federal regulatory program and a state's effort at comprehensive coastal water planning and management as part of its coastal zone management program.

During 1976, the potential hazards of tanker accidents became dramatically evident. Congressional hearings as well as new state and federal legislation followed from a major series of tanker accidents in December, 1976, and January, 1977.

1. December 15—The tanker, Argo Merchant, ran aground in Nantucket Sound and within six days had spilled 7.6 million gallons of oil.
2. December 17—The tanker, Sansinena, exploded in Los Angeles Harbor after having unloaded more than 500,000 gallons of fuel oil.
3. December 24—The tanker, Owsego Peace, spilled 2,000 gallons of oil into Thames River near Groton, Connecticut
4. December 27—The tanker, Olympic Games, ran aground in Delaware River, spilling 134,000 gallons of oil.
5. December 30—The tanker, Grand Zenith, with 8.2 million gallons of oil, disappeared 300 miles east southeast of Cape Cod.

6. January 4—The tanker, Universe Leader, with 21 million
gallons of oil, went aground off Salem, New Jersey, to
avoid a collision with the tanker Texaco California,
carrying 7 million gallons of oil.

Eighty percent of vessel casualties occur within coastal and
harbor regions, and oil spill cleanup costs are estimated at
$30,000,000-$35,000,000 per year.[1] It is a major problem that
is intensifying in severity; 1976 was a record year for oil spills.
Total oil imports to the United States are expected to increase
as much as 70% by 1980.[2]

This inevitably means more tanker traffic and an increased
danger of accidents. The size of potential oil spills has also
greatly increased. In 1955 the largest tanker afloat was the
Spyros Niarchos with a capacity of 47,470 DWT. In 1973, a
477,000-DWT tanker, Globtik Tokyo, was launched[3] and
there is a possibility that even larger tankers will be constructed.[4]
Continued reliance upon tanker transport is in part assured by
the announced intentions of Canada to cease all sales of oil or
gas to this country by 1981. This problem is not restricted to
oil tankers. There are also problems associated with the shipment of liquid natural gas (LNG) and liquid petroleum gas
(LPG), both of which represent different and in some ways
greater problems than oil. Globtik Tankers USA just recently
signed a letter of intent with the Newport News Shipbuilding
and Drydock Company for the construction of three nuclear-
powered, 600,000-DWT oil tankers. These nuclear tankers may
represent even further management issues.

CURRENT PROBLEMS

1. Some 94% of petroleum imported into the United States
is carried by foreign-fleet vessels. Many of them, under "flags
of convenience," are in questionable operating condition, often
improperly equipped, and operated by improperly trained
crew.[5] With projections of a major expansion in tanker traffic,
there is justification for the concern that present traffic control
systems may not be sufficient.

2. While energy matters are of major national and state concern, coastal waters now and in the future must meet a variety

of needs. Attempting to accommodate these other uses may be complicated by growing tanker traffic. OCS oil and gas development, deepwater ports, floating nuclear power plants and other offshore surface and submerged uses are increasing at the very time when oil imports are expected to increase. Each of the structures associated with these expanding activities represents a potential hazard to tanker traffic.

3. If an oil tanker spills its cargo, the ability to prevent that cargo from causing major water and shore damage appears still to be greatly limited, as demonstrated during the Argo Merchant spill. Further, the potential destruction of an LNG tanker is considerable. The nature and severity of these potential impacts suggest that tanker traffic may be incompatible with some other coastal uses or specific coastal natural systems.

4. Congress has declared that energy production is in the national interest. The Coastal Zone Management Act, as amended, is both implicit and explicit in suggesting that approved coastal zone management programs must provide some degree of accommodation to energy-related activities. It is unrealistic to consider the exclusion of oil or LNG tanker traffic from coastal waters. Yet any accommodation, especially during the present period of tanker traffic increase and the growing importance of coastal waters for other uses, raises a series of major problems.

5. The Coast Guard, which through the Ports and Waterways Safety Act of 1972 has principal regulatory authority over tanker safety in coastal waters, has often stated the position that unilateral tanker safety standards might harm international relations and that regulation through the Intergovernmental Maritime Consultative Organization (IMCO) or another international group might be more appropriate than attempting to set our own national standards.[6]

METHODS OF IMPROVED TANKER SAFETY

Several recent studies and reports have suggested a series of improvements in tanker construction and operation designed to decrease negative impacts of tanker traffic in coastal waters.

While there are individuals and groups who question the need, effectiveness or economic consequences of enforcing such standards, it would seem that several or most of these improvements will be required within the near future.

1. Require tankers to have double bottoms or double hulls to provide added protection against spillage if grounding or collision occurs.
2. Require inert gas systems to reduce risk of tank explosions.
3. Require segregated ballast tanks so that oil from cargo tanks is not flushed into coastal waters along with ballast waters.
4. Require better steering and propulsion systems, including double rudders and/or double boilers to provide more control and backup during equipment failure.
5. Require better navigation equipment and information.
6. Insure better training of officers and crew, perhaps through the type of testing and licensing that airline personnel must undergo.
7. Increase inspection and maintenance on tankers, especially those more than 10 years old.[4,5]

No matter how many structural or regulatory improvements are made, increased tanker traffic in crowded coastal waters will probably continue to represent a major risk to other coastal water uses.

Long-range options may exist: aside from reducing our need for imported oil and liquified gas, new transportation systems might be established, such as deepwater ports. Traffic would then be concentrated in special areas removed from high-traffic, heavy-use coastal waters. This option, which is discussed in Chapter 9, tends to shift patterns of tanker traffic rather than diminish it. However, for many coastal areas, such as Puget Sound, it may represent a reasonable alternative to increasing numbers of small- and medium-sized tankers.

But even with this type of solution, it can be expected that most coastal states will be faced with the problem of accommodating increased tanker traffic within their coastal waters in such a way as to protect the coastal zone and also allow for the expansion of other coastal uses with which tanker traffic might conflict.

EXISTING REGULATIONS

The principal regulatory authority for tanker safety in coastal waters is the Ports and Waterways Safety Act of 1972. New regulations affecting the implementation of this Act have been issued by the Coast Guard in recent years. They include:

1. "Rules for the Protection of the Marine Environment Relating to Tanker Vessels Carrying Oil in Bulk," *Federal Register* (December 13, 1976); and
2. "Navigation Safety and Vessel Inspection Regulations," *Federal Register* (January 31, 1977).

These regulations require that both foreign and domestic vessels engaged in U.S. coastal commercial trade must have segregated ballast tanks and, except under special conditions, may not carry ballast water in an oil fuel tank.

Any oil residue from tank washing must be kept in slop tanks, and discharge of this material is not allowed within 50 miles of the United States coast. These structural and operational regulations apply to all new vessels constructed after January 1, 1977. Also required under the new regulations are certain tests of vessel systems prior to entering a U.S. port, and improved navigational equipment. In future, Loran C and collision avoidance equipment may be required.

REGULATORY AUTHORITY

The Ports and Waterways Safety Act provides the U.S. Coast Guard with full authority to establish traffic regulatory systems, vessel and equipment standards, rules of operation and traffic control networks, including zones of travel, direction and speed.

Coastal states are not preempted from establishing safety regulations.

"...nor does it (Act) prevent a state or political subdivision thereof from prescribing for structures; only higher safety equipment requirements or safety standards than those which may be prescribed pursuant to this title." [Section 102(b)]

However, as discussed in Chapter 2 on Jurisdiction, there are certain rules that might affect a state's ability to establish such regulations. While this Act may not preclude stricter state regulation, the Constitution reserves for Congress affairs dealing with interstate commerce. Also, in the Coastal Zone Management Act of 1972 states are charged with giving full consideration to the "national interest" and insuring that political subdivisions of the state do not unreasonably preclude developments of regional or national benefit.

New amendments to this Act have been introduced by Representative Studds. The amendments would greatly strengthen Coast Guard authority and responsibility:

H. R. 3796: Ports and Waterways Safety Act of 1977 and Amendments

Title I

Sec. 101(a)(1) Establish, operate, and maintain vessel traffic systems of services. . . .

Sec. 101(a)(2) Require any vessel, which operates within waters subject to any vessel traffic system or service, to utilize or comply with any such system or service, including requiring the installation and use of any electronic or other device necessary for such utilization or compliance.

Sec. 101(a)(3) Control vessel traffic by:
  (a) specifying times of entry, movement, or departure; including if necessary restriction of passage to daylight hours;
  (b) establishing vessel traffic routing schemes;
  (c) establish draft, vessel size and speed limitations, and vessel operating conditions; and
  (d) restrict operation, in any hazardous area or under hazardous conditions, by any vessel which has particular operating characteristics or capabilities; in a manner deemed necessary for safe operation under the circumstances.

Sec. 101(a)(4) Direct the anchoring, mooring, or movement of any vessel when necessary to prevent damage to or by that vessel or its stores, cargo, supplies, or fuel.

Sec. 101(b) The Secretary shall establish, operate, and maintain computerized tracking and date retrieval systems as part of the vessel traffic systems which are established pursuant to subsection (a), in all ports and harbors through which pass in excess of an average of one hundred thousand barrels per day of hazardous material carried in bulk as cargo.

Sec. 102(3)   Establishing water or waterfront safety zones or other measures for limited, controlled, or conditional access and activity when necessary for the protection of any vessel, structure, waters, or shore area.

Sec. 4417a(4)   Standard-setting authority gives Secretary authority to adopt vessel standards necessary for increased navigation and vessel safety and enhanced protection of the marine environment. Minimum standards would include, after January 1, 1979:

4417a(4)(B)(5)

   (A)   a radar system with short- and long-range capabilities and with true-north features;
   (B)   a Loran C, long-range navigation aid;
   (C)   a transponder which can automatically report position and identification;
   (D)   adequate communications equipment;
   (E)   a fathometer;
   (F)   two gyrocompasses;
   (G)   up-to-date charts;
   (H)   a segregated ballast system, if such vessel carries oil in bulk and is of a size in excess of twenty thousand deadweight tons;
   (I)   a gas inerting system, if such vessel carries oil in bulk and is of a size in excess of fifty thousand deadweight tons; and
   (J)   a redundant propulsion source.

Title III: Marine Safety Authority of the United States
A 200-mile zone, seaward of the territorial sea is established:
- within which discharge of oil or hazardous material would be prohibited;
- vessel traffic control regulations might be established;
- vessels destined for United States ports might be inspected.

Sec. 403 would establish a national inspection program and insure that each vessel covered under the Act was inspected at least once each year.

It is not clear how this Act would affect state coastal water management authorities; it is an issue that requires careful attention by coastal states.

CASE HISTORY: WASHINGTON STATE

The Alaskan pipeline was scheduled to begin transporting oil from Alaska's North Slope by the summer of 1977. It is estimated that as much as 2 million gallons of oil per day will flow to Valdez where the oil will be loaded on tankers and carried to the West Coast. This represents a tremendous increase in tanker traffic, which currently carried 6.3 million gallons of oil into this country daily.[7] Because of this projected increase, Alaska has continued to urge more stringent requirements under the Ports and Waterways Safety Act[8] and Washington State, where much of the oil is scheduled to be transported, has established regulations that restrict tanker size within Puget Sound to 125,000 DWT. The Washington Act also requires that above 50,000 DWT a tanker must have:

- aboard a licensed Washington State pilot;
- specific horsepower;
- twin screws;
- double bottom; and
- two radars, including avoidance radar.

As described in Chapter 4, the Atlantic Richfield Company challenged this law in the courts, and on February 28, 1977, the U.S. Supreme Court agreed to review the case. Resolution of this case may clarify the nature of coastal state authority to regulate tanker traffic within its coastal waters.

CONCLUSIONS

The Coast Guard has considerable authority to regulate the operation and construction of tankers. However, in an effort to secure necessary control over tanker traffic, Congress may inadvertently begin to diminish the authority or management capabilities of local port authorities and state coastal zone management programs. The consistency provisions of the CZMA should assure some degree of state input into Coast Guard planning and management. But complex surface control systems such as those suggested in H.R. 3796 may in fact become the coastal water management programs for a significant portion of a state's coastal zone. The legality and impact of such federal water control systems is unclear. But at a minimum it would seem provident to require that such systems be designed and implemented on a state-federal partnership basis. Full state and local participation in all phases of the system development might be required if such water use management systems are to have any hope of being consistent with state coastal management plans. Such systems will affect regional patterns of shore and water use, and cannot just be "plugged in" to a comprehensive state management program through a reactive consistency review.

REFERENCES

1. United States Coast Guard. "Navigation Safety and Vessel Inspection Regulations," *Federal Register* (January 31, 1977).
2. Testimony of William T. Coleman, former Secretary of Transportation, before Senate Commerce Committee, January 1977 as reported in *Conservation Report* (January 21, 1977), National Wildlife Federation, Washington, D.C.
3. Department of Transportation. Final Environmental Impact/4 Statement, Loop Deepwater Port License Application, Executive Summary (1976) p. 4.
4. Mostert, Noel. *Supership.* (New York: Alfred A. Knopf, 1974).
5. Office of Technology Assessment. *Oil Transportation by Tanker,* Washington, D.C. (July 1975) p. 19.
6. Siler, Admiral Owen, U.S. Coast Guard. *Conservation Report* (January 21, 1977) p. 22.
7. Kifner, J. "Flag-of-Convenience Oil Tankers," *New York Times* (February 13, 1977).
8. *Conservation News* (January 21, 1977) p. 22.

CHAPTER 9

LIQUEFIED NATURAL GAS

Principal Agencies: U.S. Coast Guard (DOT)
        Federal Energy Regulatory Commission (DOE)
         (formerly Federal Power Commission)
        Office of Pipeline Safety Operations (DOT)
Principal Legislation: Natural Gas Pipeline Safety Act of 1968
        Ports and Waterways Safety Act of 1972
        Coastal Zone Management Act of 1972
        Dangerous Cargo Act of 1970

The principal reason for liquefying natural gas is to reduce its volume for transport and storage. When natural gas is cooled to 259° below zero F, it is compressed into a clear liquid 1/600 its original size. 600 cubic feet of natural gas condenses into one cubic foot of liquid. Liquefied Petroleum Gas (LPG), butadine, anhydrous ammonia, propylene and vinyl chloride are some of the other gases that are commonly liquefied by exposure to low temperatures, high pressures, or both.[1]

The major danger of LNG occurs when and if it is released from its insulated storage tank and exposed to ambient air temperatures and/or water. It rapidly vaporizes, can cause a flameless explosion, and may spread as a vapor cloud into populated areas of fuel storage areas. The greatest damage occurs when and if this vapor is ignited. The flame can travel back to the leaking tank, generating intense heat and flames.

INCREASED LNG SHIPMENTS

Interest in importing larger amounts of LNG into the United States has grown during the last 10 years. At present major expansions in LNG tanker capacity are taking place. The average capacity of the 35 LNG tankers now in operation is 46,000 cubic meters of liquid. There are 41 other LNG tankers under construction or in the design stage, and their mean capacity is 124,000 cubic meters, with plans for larger ships with a capacity up to 165,000 cubic meters.[2]

The United States currently exports more LNG than it imports. While 10.8 trillion Btu's of LNG were imported to Massachusetts from Algeria in 1976, 32 trillion Btu's of LNG were shipped to Japan from Alaskan fields,[3] but this balance is expected to shift rapidly. The primary use of LNG in the United States has been as a source of peak-demand fuel by municipal gas companies. But with depletion of United States gas stocks, LNG is increasingly proposed as a baseload fuel, which would require a major expansion in importations. This trend is reflected in the changing size of land storage tanks, which previously had been typically of 50,000 cubic meter capacity. Two new controversial storage tanks in Newark, New Jersey, are 14 stories high each and have a designed capacity of 38 million gallons of LNG apiece.

THE ISSUES

Many coastal states can expect to be faced with management issues related to LNG shipments or storage. If there is a pipeline, tanker or storage tank accident, a flameless vapor explosion could occur as the liquefied natural gas hits the water. If a spill is ignited, it burns like gasoline. If it is not ignited quickly, the vapor may be blown into populated areas or fuel storage facilities and then ignited. Once ignited, a flame front burns back through the vapor to the source.

> The sudden destruction of a tank containing liquefied natural gas would be expected to lead to a major fire with potential disastrous consequences.[3]

Substantial improvements in design and safety planning have been made since a major 1944 Cleveland LNG fire, in part as a result of work done by NASA and DOD on liquefied rocket fuels. At the present time, more than 60 LNG facilities exist in the United States and Canada, with an excellent safety record. However, if an accident occurs, the potential for death and destruction is extraordinary.

PRESENT SAFEGUARDS

The Coast Guard has established several types of regulations for LNG shipments and is developing more. Coast Guard regulations fall within two categories: (a) design and construction standards for LNG vessels, and (b) operational controls on LNG vessels while entering, moored or leaving U.S. ports.

Design and Construction

LNG represents special problems as it can cause structural damage to a vessel if it is spilled upon the deck or hull, due to its extremely cold temperature. The liquid can burn human flesh, and is a major fire hazard once released into the environment. Standards that have been developed by the Intergovernmental Maritime Consultative Organization (IMCO), the Coast Guard's Chemical Transportation Industry Advisory Committee (CTIAC), and Coast Guard personnel are now leading to several revisions in international and U.S. codes.

The Coast Guard feels that these new standards provide a "consistent and reasonable level of safety for the containment and transportation of LNG."[4]

> In general, the vessels are designed to survive two-compartment flooding from collision or stranding with reserve stability. These vessels, as with other merchant vessels, are not designed to withstand a major collision or stranding without cargo release, but the design does limit the release to the tanks directly involved in the incident.[5]

Typical of present LNG vessel design is a tanker under construction at the Quincy Shipbuilding Division of the General Dynamics Corporation. It consists of five spherical LNG storage tanks, each with a capacity of 25,000 cubic feet. Each tank is shielded and segregated, so that in an accident it is hoped that at most, one tank would be ruptured. Because of American harbor depth limitations, most LNG tankers will be limited to a 125,000 cubic meter capacity, with a length of 900 feet, a 150-foot beam and a depth of 80 feet.

Operational Controls

The Coast Guard has statutory authority to regulate port safety under 50 U.S.C. 191, Executive Order 10173, and the Ports and Waterways Safety Act of 1972. There are no specific regulations for LNG facilities under the Ports and Waterways Safety Act at the present time, but they may soon be promulgated. The Coast Guard Captain of the Port (COTP) can require a Coast Guard escort, a sliding safety zone around the LNG tanker, movement only during good weather and other conditions.

The March 17, 1977, *Federal Register* contains a proposed amendment to the Ports and Waterways Safety Act regulations to specifically allow the designation of safety zones, either fixed or sliding. This Act also recognizes the authority of coastal states to develop more stringent controls, although that concept is now facing review by the U.S. Supreme Court in the Washington State ARCO dispute (*Ray v. Atlantic Richfield Company*).

COASTAL MANAGEMENT CONSIDERATIONS

Jurisdiction

The Coast Guard currently claims full jurisdiction over the entire shore terminal, including storage tanks, loading and offloading equipment, pipelines from the terminal and the vessel:

> In other words, the entire portion of the LNG system that connects the cryogenic tanker to the distribution system is of concern to the Coast Guard.[6]

Also included in Coast Guard jurisdiction is the movement of LNG tankers within U.S. waters, especially port areas. But the Ports and Waterways Safety Act is quite specific (Section 102(b)) in recognizing state authority to also establish "higher safety equipment requirements or safety standards" than the Coast Guard may establish. Also, Section 104 of the PWSA requires that the Coast Guard provide states with "an adequate opportunity for consultation and comment" prior to establishing rules, regulations and standards.

However, as discussed in Chapter 8, there are complicating factors of interstate commerce that might weaken the ability of a state to establish its own regulations. In any instance, each coastal state and local port authority retains considerable responsibilities, especially for facility security.

Security

Accidents, terrorist activities, sabotage or vandalism could lead to major coastal destruction if some part of an LNG terminal/vessel system were ruptured or tampered with. There are few coastal facilities that demand greater security measures, if an appropriate degree of public safety is to be provided.

> Facilities handling LNG are required to practice strict security
> measures in order to insure safety of the facility and the port.[8]

This security is primarily a local or state, rather than Coast Guard responsibility, although significant Coast Guard/state/local coordination is necessary in all aspects of LNG management.

Fire Planning

The Captain of each port in which LNG is handled will develop and implement his own LNG contingency plan. This will require assistance from the local fire marshall as well as the regional emergency planning officer or state police. Special insurance considerations may be involved, not only for the facility, but also for adjacent property, and this way may have significant impacts upon the immediate vicinity in terms of costs or special safeguards.

Facility Siting

The Federal Energy Regulatory Commission (formerly the Federal Power Commission), under authority of the Natural Gas Act of 1938 and the Department of Energy Organization Act of 1977 has a degree of permit authority over LNG facilities in its issuance of certificates of public convenience and necessity. The Corps of

Engineers through Section 10 and Section 404 permits can influence LNG siting decisions. And the Coast Guard, under authority of the Ports and Waterways Safety Act, can influence the location of both shore facilities and water transport corridors, and any associated water-based facilities. States, under authority of the Coastal Zone Management Act, and both state and local governments, under broad "police powers," have considerable influence over various aspects of siting, although the degree of actual control is not clear. Any attempt by a state coastal zone management program to develop LNG siting criteria and procedures may be complicated by this unclear distribution of authority. Yet is is important that LNG facilities be sited with care. A single clear coordinated regulatory program might insure such care.

An example of why there can and should be both concern and careful siting criteria for LNG facilities is provided by a fuel barge fire that occurred in Mobile Harbor in February of 1977. The towboat, W. F. Fredeman, Jr., was moving four barges loaded with 109,000 barrels of naptha from a Mobile harbor refinery when one of the barges hit a pylon of a bridge and exploded. Luckily, the other barges did not explode. But a fireboat from the City of Mobile and three Coast Guard vessels spent some eight hours before the fire was extinguished.

As reported in *National Fisherman*, there was considerable danger that the burning barge and flaming fuel on the water might have floated down on several fuel storage facilities located merely yards downstream. It could have been "a major waterfront disaster" if the flames had ignited any of the fuel stored at the shore facilities. Hard work by the boat crews and favorable tide and wind conditions were the main reasons why it was not a major accident. If the spill had involved the rupture of a 25,000 cubic meter LNG tank, the results might have been far worse.[7]

COASTAL PLANNING FOR LNG FACILITIES

Advocates of increased LNG shipment and storage in U.S. coastal regions emphasize the good safety record of present LNG facilities and operations, and of the increasingly strict construction and operational standards being developed. However, LNG remains a particularly difficult substance and set of activities to accommodate. As the Coast Guard has observed, LNG is:

> A hazardous commodity, although not the most dangerous being shipped today. It is precisely because of the danger of this cargo that first the Coast Guard, and then others have studied this material.[8]

Given the dangers and in some instances community resistence to LNG facilities and shipments, siting is increasingly difficult. The Coast guard can provide technical assistance, but as a policy, relies upon local regulations to establish most of the actual land use siting criteria.

COASTAL DEPENDENCY

Baseload LNG facilities are highly coastal dependent. The reasons for this are discussed in the *Massachusetts Coastal Zone Management Preview*:

> While it is technically feasible to site a (LNG) facility inland, away from the marine terminal throughwhich the LNG is imported, the expense involved would be prohibitive. In addition, using a cryogenic pipeline running from the marine terminal to inland storage tanks would increase the probability of an LNG accident. The coastal dependency of baseload LNG facilities thus limits available alternatives.[9]

For the same reason, offshore facilities are in most instances impractical. Because of the hazard of the material, a pipeline rupture from a dragged anchor or other cause might represent an unacceptable risk to human safety and marine life. In addition, the cost of special cryogenic pipelines would make such an arrangement much more costly than an equivalent oil storage facility.

Siting restrictions such as avoidance of fault zones and avoidance of high population areas are some obvious concerns, and there may not be any fully acceptable site. Rural communities may be no more receptive to the appearance and potential hazards of LNG facilities than their urban neighbors. Extensive shore and water modification may be necessary to accommodate LNG tankers and support facilities in rural coastal areas.

The accommodation of LNG shipments and storage within the coastal zone is an extreme example of a more general management problem of dealing with an activity that tends to be incompatible with other uses and that, while necessary, is not really welcomed. Such activities generate strong political opposition and defy simple management solutions. Given these difficulties, it is interesting to consider the approach of Massachusetts' and California's CZMP toward LNG management.

CALIFORNIA MANAGEMENT OF LNG FACILITIES

In 1976, the State of California adopted the California Coastal Act (SB 1277), which is the principal mechanism for the state's coastal zone management program. In that Act is a specific policy regarding LNG facilities, which is self-explanatory and is quoted in full, as follows:

> Section 30261(b): Only *one liquefied natural gas terminal shall be permitted in the coastal zone* until engineering and operational practices can eliminate any significant risk to life due to accident or until guaranteed supplies of liquefied natural gas and distribution system dependence on liquefied natural gas are substantial enough that an interruption of service from a single liquefied natural gas facility would not cause substantial public harm.

> Until the risks inherent in liquefied natural gas terminal operations can be sufficiently identified and overcome and such terminals are found to be consistent with the health and safety of nearby human populations, terminals shall be built only at sites remote from human population concentrations. Other unrelated development in the vicinity of a liquefied natural gas terminal site which is remote from human population concentrations shall be prohibited. At such time as liquefied natural gas marine terminal operations are found consistent with public safety, terminal sites only in developed or industrialized port areas may be approved. (emphasis added)

In September 1977 this approach was modified by the passage of California Senate Bill 1081, titled the *Liquefied Natural Gas Terminal Act of 1977*. This act placed more emphasis upon a positive program to seek out possible LNG facility onshore and offshore sites. The California Public Utilities Commission is given exclusive permit powers for LNG facilities, with the California Coastal Commission charged with making recommendations on potential sites to the PUC. Population density remains the principal factor in siting. Of particular interest is Sec. 5582(3) which specifies that LNG terminals should be located so that the path of marine vessels carrying LNG will also avoid major population areas. This suggests the establishment of water zones based upon adjacent land conditions (population density), which is a strategy that may take on increasing importance in coastal water management.

MASSACHUSETTS LNG POLICY

Massachusetts has not ruled out expanded LNG facilities, but has articulated certain siting criteria. New or expanded baseload LNG facilities are to be approved at existing sites only if:

1. existing facilities cannot accommodate additional throughput;
2. environmental assessments indicate that public safety risks and environmental damage would be less than accommodating larger deliveries or new facilities elsewhere.

Additionally,

3. tanks must be sited away from areas of high population densities;
4. design and operation shall reflect the highest state-of-the-art;
5. dikes must be able to contain any LNG which might escape;
6. adequate buffer zones must be provided in order to protect the public from dangers associated with a spill.[10]

CONCLUSIONS

The U.S. Coast Guard, the Federal Energy Regulatory Commission (DOE), and the Office of Pipeline Safety Operations (DOT) all have some degree of jurisdiction over LNG facilities and operations. The multiple federal interests and agencies with sometimes unclear or conflicting authority make it difficult not only for private industry but also for state coastal management programs to maintain an effective management interface with federal regulatory and policy activities. Also, it is not clear as to how much control state coastal management programs can have over LNG facility policies and regulations. The Coast Guard in particular has relied upon a cooperative management structure that involves not only the coast guard and the LNG companies, but also state and local governmental cooperation. However, as new centralized national energy programs emerge under the Department of Energy, and as the potential for conflict between state coastal management programs and federal energy or facilities siting policy increases, it is possible that federal preemption, perhaps under authority of the Commerce Clause of the Constitution, may be evoked.

LNG is only one of several hazardous or toxic materials that must increasingly receive special attention in coastal planning, for both land and water areas. The need to protect human population concentrations and valuable natural systems from possible LNG accidents or acts of sabotage suggests the need for careful siting of both transportation and storage systems away from flood areas, earthquakes, hurricane paths, crowded waterways, other explosive or flammable substances, and where appropriate security can be maintained. Special attention should be given to the coastal *water* facilities and LNG marine vessel corridors. Special *hazardous shipment water zones* may be required, as well as other water use management techniques.

Under 1976 amendments to the Coastal Zone Management Act, Sec. 305(b)(8) requires that be October 1978 each state program must include:

> A planning process for energy facilities likely to be located in, or which may significantly affect, the coastal zone, including, but not limited to, a process for anticipating and managing the impacts from such facilities.

Sec. 304(b)(5) of the amended Coastal Zone Management Act specifically identifies "facilities used for the transportation, conversion, treatment, transfer, or storage of liquefied natural gas" as being "energy facilities" as mentioned in Section 305. Therefore, the Coastal Zone Management Act now provides not only a mechanism, but a specific program requirement through which coastal states can develop plans and management approaches to the problems of liquefied natural gas.

The impact of these provisions is not yet clear. The U.S. Coast Guard, the Federal Energy Regulatory Commission and

the Office of Pipeline Safety Operations currently administer
LNG planning and regulatory programs. The Coastal Zone Management Act amendments of 1976 provide a mechanism for
coordinating all of these state and federal interests into a comprehensive and united management approach. But the presence
of federal interests also represents potential problems of coordination and consistency. While Sec. 305 (b) (8) gives coastal
states clear authority to develop management plans for coastal
LNG facilities, it is not clear as to what actual *regulatory authority* the states maintain, given a strong federal interest in the
energy, commerce and navigation aspects of LNG activities.

In May 1977, Representative Dingell (D-Michigan) introduced
H.R. 6844 (Liquefied Natural Gas Facility Safety Act). This
legislation would provide the Secretary of Transportation with
full permit authority over all LNG facilities (Sec. 5).

Section 7 (a) (1) stipulates that this Act would not preempt
state authority to regulate LNG facilities. However, it also requires that state actions be compatible with federal standards
established under the act.

> A State or political subdivision thereof shall not be preempted
> under this Act from adopting, enforcing, or continuing in effect
> any provision of law or regulation establishing standards with
> respect to liquefied natural gas facilities unless such standards
> are incompatible with the standards under this Act.

The placement of such authority with the Secretary of Transportation may be inconsistent with the recently established Department of Energy, which has a mandate to centralize within
a single department all energy-related planning and management.
Also of importance is the absence within H.R. 6844 (May 1977
draft) of any specific reference to state coastal zone management programs. There is a potential conflict between H.R.
6844 and Section 305 (b) (8) and the Section 307 consistency
provisions of the Coastal Zone Management Act. As with many
other coastal management issues, it is not clear as to whether
the states or federal authorities will be given the right to evoke
consistency.

Reflecting a growing Congressional interest in LNG issues, and
also as a result of a specific LNG facility proposed for Prudence

Island in Narragansett Bay, Rhode Island, Senator Claiborne Pell (D-RI), in November 1977 introduced a *Liquefied Natural Gas Siting and Safety Act.* This legislation would place LNG regulatory authority within the Department of Energy. Also, this legislation gives specific recognition to state concerns and state coastal management programs, and provides that if a state rejects a particular LNG proposal, the Secretary of the Department of Energy can override the state rejection only "in the interest of national security" [Sec. 5 (f)].

With projections and proposals for significant increases in the importation of LNG, formal and comprehensive coastal LNG policies and regulations will be required. However, within the perspective of coastal water management, LNG is but one of many pressing management issues, and shares many management elements with more general concerns about hazardous materials and siting policy for any major facility within coastal areas. It is hoped that this commonality will be recognized in future federal and state legislation. It is also hoped that LNG management will not be totally removed from coastal management programs, but retained as part of a comprehensive coastal resource management effort.

REFERENCES

1. Coast Guard. *Liquefied Natural Gas: Views and Practices, Policy and Safety* (February 1976), p. II-1.
2. Drake, E. and R. C. Reid. "The Importation of Liquefied Natural Gas" *Scientific American* (April 1977), p. 24.
3. *Ibid.,* p. 22.
4. *Ibid.,* p. 29.
5. U.S. Coast Guard. *Liquefied Natural Gas: Views and Practices, Policy and Safety* (February 1976), p. III-12.
6. *Ibid.,* p. IV-4.
7. Norville, W. "Heroic Small Boat Effort Stifles Mobile Catastrophe," *National Fisherman* (April 1977), p. 24-A.
8. U.S. Coast Guard. *Liquefied Natural Gas: Views and Practices, Policy and Safety* (February 1976), p. II-8.
9. Executive Office of Environmental Affairs. *Massachusetts Coastal Zone Management Preview* (November 1976), p. 2-G/11.
10. *Ibid.,* p. 2-G/25.

RECOMMENDED READINGS

Department of Transportation, U.S. Coast Guard, *The Port of Boston LNG LPG-Operation/Emergency Plan.* Boston. March 1977.

Dingell, Representative John D. (D-Mich.). *Liquefied Natural Gas Facility Safety Act (H.R. 6844)* May 3, 1977.

Office of Technology Assessment. *Transportation of Liquefied Natural Gas.* September 1977. U.S. Government Printing Office.

Pell, Senator Claiborne (D- Rhode Island). *Liquefied Natural Gas Siting and Safety Act (S. 2273)* November 1, 1977.

State of California. *Liquefied Natural Gas Terminal Act of 1977* S.B. 1081, September 17, 1977.

U.S. Department of Transportation, Office of Pipeline Safety Operations. "Liquefied Natural Gas Facilities (LNG); Federal Safety Standards," *Federal Register* 42(77), April 21, 1977.

CHAPTER 10

OCS OIL AND GAS DEVELOPMENT

Principal Agencies: Bureau of Land Management (Interior)
U.S. Geological Survey (Interior)
Coast Guard (Transportation)
Office of Pipeline Safety (Transportation)
Department of Energy

Principal Legislation: Outer Continental Shelf Lands Act
Federal Water Pollution Control Act
Amendments of 1972
National Environmental Policy Act

In the United States, growing pressure to lease outer continental shelf (OCS) submerged lands for expanded oil and gas production has led to increased state and local concern over possible coastal impacts, including possible spills and intensified demand for public services. A 1977 Phillips platform blowout in the North Sea only heightened that concern.

By 1974, more than 17,000 wells had been drilled in the coastal and ocean waters of the United States. However, more than 95% of this OCS production had occurred off the coast of Louisiana. Most states, faced for the first time with potential OCS leases in frontier areas, have little experience with oil and gas planning and management. Further, the reasonable safety record for the Gulf of Mexico may not be a proper indication of conditions and problems to be found in Alaskan or North Atlantic waters. Final impacts are still unknown.

This chapter attempts to describe some possible coastal water impacts of OCS development, the present distribution of jurisdictional authority, and proposed changes in basic federal legislation. The regulatory framework for the planning and management of OCS oil and gas development is rapidly changing, after many years as a relatively static system. For those interested in this topic, it will be particularly important to monitor pending legislation and regulations, which may well be enacted during 1978.

OCS IMPACTS ON COASTAL WATERS

Much attention has been given to the onshore impacts of OCS development. The Coastal Energy Impact Program (CEIP) established under Sec. 308 of the Coastal Zone Management Act of 1976, provides coastal states with financial assistance to deal with these impacts. It can be expected that OCS developments may also have direct and significant impacts upon coastal waters:

1. *Increased surface traffic.* Various types of vessels will travel to and from OCS lease sites. If a major field is involved, this might represent a significant increase in traffic, especially in or near urban areas, recreational sites, or fishing ports.

2. *Increased subsurface hazards.* A majority of oil pipeline spills have been caused by accidents such as anchor dragging. As the number of pipelines from OCS areas and/or deepwater ports increases, state and federal agencies will not only have to insure that they are properly marked on navigation charts, but that other uses of coastal waters do not damage these systems.
   However, oil and gas development can also be expected to lead to other obstacles. Some areas of the North Sea seabed look "like a forest of steel."[1] Debris includes, aside from 'normal' shipboard waste, pipes, hawsers, cement blocks, and other drilling-related materials. Trawls can be damaged or destroyed, and future uses may be limited or precluded, unless great care is taken.

3. *Loss of fish habitat.* As pipeline is laid, bottom habitat may be damaged or destroyed. Dredging, spoil disposal, or oil spills may directly damage marine life, especially in the early stages of life, or may damage habitat areas.

4. *Increasing law enforcement problems.* Expanded offshore development will lead to an increased need for property protection and law enforcement. It is not always clear who has policing authority or who should absorb the often considerable costs of such actions. Coastal managers should work closely with state and local police as well as the Coast Guard.

POSITIVE IMPACTS

Much of the literature regarding OCS development and the provisions of the CEIP program of the amended Coastal Zone Management Act emphasize possible negative impacts resulting from oil and gas activities. While such concerns are important, they could obscure the fact that increased OCS activity may also have several positive impacts upon coastal areas, including improved tax base, new employment, or needed improvement in public services. It is important to remember that coastal management includes use as well as protection. States should not only be concerned about preventing negative impacts, but also should attempt to take advantage of any opportunities. Thus OCS activities suggest a need to integrate within coastal land and water planning economic development considerations, public facilities improvements, employment opportunities, the prevention of oil spills, development of pipeline corridors, and appropriate patterns of land or water use. However, it then becomes necessary to consider whether or not states currently have sufficient authority to effect such integration. Previously, OCS leasing has been considered as being primarily a federal rather than a state activity. Consequently, states have encountered a historic difficulty in gaining a voice in the decision process, or in obtaining necessary management information. But this trend appears to be changing, in proposed amendments to the Outer Continental Shelf Lands Act, to be described below, and in provisions of the Coastal Zone Management Act.

FEDERAL AUTHORITY

The Outer Continental Shelf Lands Act of 1953 gave full authority to the Secretary of Interior to lease OCS submerged lands, and directs the Secretary to expedite oil and gas production as being in the national interest (see Chapter 2).

The administration of energy-related activities in the oceans
and coastal waters is now in a time of change. Previously, OCS
authority had been divided within the Department of Interior
between the Bureau of Land Management (BLM) and the United
States Geologic Survey (USGS). The Department of Energy
Organization Act of 1977 has modified the role of interior, in
that many of the functions previously held by BLM are now
administered by the Department of Energy. Future modifications
in this allocation of authority are probable, in pending amendments to the OCSLA. But it would seem that at least for the
present, once a decision has been made to lease OCS lands, the
USGS still has responsibility for development and production of
the leases. USGS administers its authority through Area Oil
and Gas Supervisors.

> The supervisor . . . shall inspect and regulate all operations
> and is authorized to issue OCS orders and other orders and
> rules necessary for him to effectively supervise operations
> and to prevent damage to or waste of, any natural resource,
> or injury to life or property. The supervisor shall receive,
> and shall, when in his judgement it is necessary, consult with
> or solicit advice from lessees, field officials or interested
> Departments and agencies . . . and representatives of state
> and local government. (Sec. 250.12)

The principal method of regulating OCS activities is through
a set of orders for each USGS region, although it appears that
USGS is now also working on a national system of orders.
Six major studies of USGS OCS regulations have been made
since 1970, as well as reviews and comments upon those studies.
These are summarized, with major findings, in Volume Two of
the OTA report on OCS impacts.[2]

OCS ORDERS

There are 15 orders that cover all phases of exploration, development, production and transportation of OCS oil and gas.
Not all these orders have been prepared for all regions, but
with one exception, they contain the same type of regulation
within each region. The type of information contained in each
order includes:

Order No. 1:   Marking of Wells, Platforms and Fixed Structures

Order No. 2:   Drilling Procedures

Order No. 3:   Plugging and Abandonment of Wells

Order No. 4:   Suspensions and Determination of Well
                  Producibility

Order No. 5:   Installation of Subsurface Safety Device

Order No. 6:   Procedure for Completion of Oil and Gas Wells

Order No. 7:   Pollution and Waste Disposal

Order No. 8:   Approval Procedure for Installation and Oper-
                  ation of Platforms, Fixed and Mobile Structures,
                  and Artificial Islands

Order No. 9:   Approval Procedures for Pipelines

Order No. 10:   Sulfur Drilling Procedures off Louisiana and
                  Texas (limited to Gulf of Mexico)

Order No. 11:   Oil and Gas Production Rates, Prevention of
                  Waste and Protection of Correlative Rights

Order No. 12:   Public Inspection of Records

Order No. 13:   Production, Measurement, and Commingling

Order No. 14:   Approval of Suspensions of Production

Order No. 15:   (no title) State's Right to OCS Information

The OTA study suggests that these orders have undergone review and improvement, but that in some instances their degree of specificity is still questionable.[2]   When compared with U.S. Coast Guard regulations for deepwater ports, the USGS orders may not be fully adequate.

Additional principal federal authorities over OCS operations include: EPA, CEQ and the Coast Guard for the National Contingency Plan and other provisions of Sec. 311 of the Federal Water Pollution Control Act; the Corps of Engineers for dredge or fill or navigation matters; and the Coast Guard for navigation and enforcement.   The specific authorities for pipelines are discussed below.

STATE AUTHORITY

The Submerged Lands Act and the Outer Continental Shelf Lands Act clearly establish that coastal states do not have authority over OCS leasing in any direct sense.   *The U.S. v. Maine* decision (see Chapter 2) further clarified this, and the Office of

Coastal Zone Management, in its threshold papers, has declared that OCS areas will not be included within the management boundary of a state's coastal zone.

> Irrespective of any extended seaward jurisdiction which may be enacted by law or agreed to under international convention, *states may not include* waters beyond the territorial sea, in the absence of specific legislation.[3]

This is consistent with the ruling of the Department of Justice and the resultant policy of OCZM that federally owned lands would be excluded from the land portion of a state's coastal management zone.

However, as with excluded federal lands, the *impacts* of OCS activities upon a state's coastal waters, to the degree that they are direct and significant, are of concern to the state and fall under the consistency provisions of the Coastal Zone Management Act.

As a general observation, the state, and local units of government beneath it, have an opportunity to influence OCS development. The new Sec. 307 provisions of the CZMA call for major state review of Interior's regulations and leasing, and recognizes a limited veto power held by thes tates if OCS activities are clearly inconsistent with an approved state CZMP. States can establish oil spill liability laws (discussed below), control the location of pipelines within state waters, regulate where they will come ashore, and establish other necessary safety measures. State tax law, although somewhat restricted, might be used to create a preferred pattern and location of oil- and gas-related development. Local government, through zoning and land use planning, under authority of delegated police powers from the state, can have major impact upon OCS development, in effect establishing where oil and gas may or may not come ashore. However, it is not clear whether a state could totally preclude the use of state waters and submerged lands for OCS-related activities.

LOCAL AUTHORITY

The 1976 amendments of the Coastal Zone Management Act included a new recognition of the need for local government to be informed of state coastal management decisions, and to consider local zoning and planning in such decisions [Sec. 306 (c) (2) (B)]. Under these new provisions, any local government whose zoning authority would be affected by a proposed state program decision must be given 30-day notification and an opportunity to comment. This should enable local governmental units to maintain a good idea of pending OCS-related activities and provide an opportunity for an expression of local concerns and needs.

However, there is also a possibility that local government may, through its zoning authority, block OCS-related activities that are otherwise consistent with a state's program. This is in fact more than a possibility, and often with good reason. As Massachusetts observed in its *Offshore Oil Development* handbook:

> . . . the real long-range benefits accrue all too often to the region or the nation, in terms of a more secure supply of energy, while the immediate costs may be borne by the locality in the form of increased public service demands, increased levels of pollution and congestion, and a loss of visual quality.[4]

Coastal water developments may provide desirable types, rates and levels of physical and economic development for communities. However, it is the coastal community that also faces the major burden of supporting coastal water development. These communities may be required to devote increasing amounts of time, money and energy to planning and managing coastal water development. Some coastal communities might therefore question OCS developments or use local authority to block terminals, pipelines or other coastal water-related facilities.

In recognition of this possibility, the Coastal Zone Management Act requires that an approved state program contain a method of assuring that local land and water use regulations within the coastal zone do not "unreasonably" restrict or exclude land and water uses of regional benefit [Sec. 306 (e) (2)]. However, there are certain conceptual and political, as well as administrative problems with attempting to provide such assurance. First, this provision may tend to dissociate the individual community from the region of which it is a part.   If the collective interest of the communities within a region is not the regional interest, then who, actually, determines the regional interest?   Unless there is some truly representative and well-functioning mechanism to articulate the regional interest, the true interests of coastal communities within a region might not be represented.   Secondly, many coastal states have placed considerable emphasis upon local planning and management as part of their coastal zone management programs.   Unless these local government units are provided some convincing degree of participation in final allocative decisions regarding coastal water activities, they may be less than cooperative in other aspects of the state program.

An Example: Orleans, Cape Cod, Massachusetts

Under Chapter 164 of the General Laws of Massachusetts, the state has established an Energy Facilities Siting Counsel (MGLA Ch. 164, S. 69G-R).   The Council is given jurisdiction over the siting of electric generating, gas and oil facilities.   The Council has broad powers to regulate energy-related facilities, and under certain circumstances can exercise powers of eminent domain.   Some citizens have perhaps correctly perceived this as a potential threat to local control of community land and water use.

Orleans is a small but growing rural community on the lower Cape, adjacent to the Cape Cod National Seashore.   It experiences a substantial seasonal population increase during the summer months and its economy is based in large part upon recreational activities.   In the spring of 1977, a proposal was made to modify Sec. 3.11 of Orleans' bylaw to preclude storage tanks for offshore oil or gas, pipelines, service facilities or helicopter ports.   Orleans retains the traditional New England Town Meeting process of local government, and the list of prohibited uses was proposed for community vote at the annual Town Meeting in May.   The article passed by a vote of 200 to 39 on May 3, 1977.[5]

In arguing for passage of the article, a local resident articulated the concern of many coastal communities, and clearly indicated the intention of the article to block possible onshore facilities intended to support OCS development.

> The only intent of this article is to throw any stumbling block in front of oil companies that might want to move in here and take over.[6]

POWER OF LOCAL GOVERNMENT

On February 17, 1977, Federal District Court Judge Jack B. Weinstein enjoined further activity on the mid-Atlantic OCS leases granted in August of 1976. This ruling, which Interior Secretary Cecil Andrus appealed, was based in part upon the Judge's finding that former Interior Secretary Thomas Kleppe, in granting the leases, had ignored the practical effects of local governmental licensing, permitting and review powers.[7] Earlier, representatives from communities in New Jersey and Long Island had indicated their intent to use local authority to block pipelines and other OCS-related facilities. While those advocating OCS development may see such obstructions as counter to the national interest, many state programs are placing strong reliance upon local planning and management, and the national interest must derive in part from citizens living within affected communities.

Most if not all coastal water and deep ocean activities require shore access. Yet the shore is not merely a point of accommodation for water-oriented activities. It is also the site of traditional land and water patterns and existent communities, often possessing fragile social, financial and environmental characteristics. OCS development is a local/state/federal partnership, each party having legitimate needs and interests, and each with recognized authority and responsibilities under the law. Federal agencies may find it difficult to deal with a large number of individual communities and may seek state coordination, and local communities may require state guidance as to how to deal with federal agencies. Furthermore, the state is faced with the task of determining the overall 'best use' pattern of the state's coastal waters and adjacent shoreland, beyond the perspective of a single community or a federal leasing policy. Implementing the provisions of Sec. 306 (e) (2) of the CZMA to the satisfaction of both local and federal interests may be one of the more difficult tasks of a state coastal management program.

ENVIRONMENTAL IMPACTS OF OIL SPILLS

Some reports on the impacts of OCS development have concluded that oil spills are more a public nuisance than a matter of major consequence.

> Large spills from OCS operations are less of a problem than smaller, more frequent spills and chronic discharges . . . Local impacts from a large spill might be quite severe, but most indications are that the major effects are short-term in nature. The marine environment is resilient and has the ability to absorb oil spill impacts through natural processes.[8]

In the past this resiliency theory of the ocean and coastal waters has led to ocean dumping, wetland destruction and other activities that are now increasingly being questioned. During war and because of past tanker and oil production operations, a great amount of oil has been discharged into the world's oceans with little detectable long-range effect. However, it seems at best premature to claim that the marine environment is resilient enough to absorb oil spill impacts without effect. Perhaps of greater importance, oil spills represent a hazard, a nuisance and a very significant cost to all coastal water activities. None of these activities are enhanced by the presence of oil spills, and some may be totally preempted when and if oil is present in significant amounts on or in the water.

MAJOR OIL SPILLS

Two recent oil spills, one from the Argo Merchant in December of 1976 and the other from the Bravo-14 well in the North Sea in April of 1977, demonstrate that predicting the outcome of a major spill is difficult. Temperature, wave height, wind velocity and direction, currents, type of oil and size of spill are all contributing factors determining the eventual effect of the spill. As in the two examples cited, it may be that most of the oil will congeal and be dispersed by wave action, moved away from shore by wind, tide and current, and actually leave little visible sign of its passage.

However, when considering the total range of possible impacts from a major oil spill, including the degree to which a wide range of coastal activities might be disrupted or displaced, it seems realistic to state, as Massachusetts has estimated, that it "could have tremendous economic and environmental impacts."[9] The Office of Coastal Zone Management has also estimated that "a variety of adverse environmental impacts can be expected in the course of OCS oil and gas development activities."

> While some of the activities would have minor or short term-impacts, others, such as the dredging and filling of wetlands, air and water pollution from refinery operations, and chronic oil pollution can be expected to cause serious environmental damage over extended periods of time.[10]

The amount of available information on oil spills is extensive. Initial information can be obtained from *Coastal Management Aspects of OCS Oil and Gas Developments* (OCZM, 1975), *Coastal Effects of Offshore Energy Systems* (OTA, 1976), and *Effects of Offshore Oil and Natural Gas Development on the Coastal Zone* (Congressional Research Service, 1976). Several states have begun to compile extensive information, such as Massachusetts' *Offshore Oil Development* (1976). OCZM has recently published a *Coastal Zone Management Annotated Bibliography* (1977) which provides access to other state studies. Also, Sea Grant programs, oceanographic research centers such as Woods Hole, and several federal agencies, including EPA and National Marine Fisheries Service, have conducted or are conducting oil spill-related studies.

OIL SPILL LIABILITY

There are several federal and state programs to insure that those suffering damages or costs as a result of an oil spill can receive some degree of compensation. Provisions also exist to insure public recovery of costs incurred in oil spill cleanups.

Federal Programs

The Federal Water Pollution Control Act (Sec. 311), the Deepwater Port Act and the Trans-Alaska Pipeline Act each establish funds to cover costs of oil spills. Proposed amendments to the Outer Continental Shelf Lands Act (H.R. 1614, H.R. 935) would establish another oil spill liability system, further complicating the federal system.

In an effort to consolidate all of these programs, Rep. Gerry Studds (D–Mass.) has introduced H.R. 2365, the Comprehensive Oil Pollution Liability and Compensation Act of 1977. This act would establish a single and all-inclusive compensation fund to pay for all removal costs and other damages resulting from oil discharge. It would consolidate all present or proposed oil spill funds, and establish a single fund of between $150 million and $200 million, financed by a three cents per barrel fee. It would specifically amend the Trans-Alaska Pipeline Authorization Act (87 Stat. 586), the Deepwater Port Act of 1974 (88 Stat. 2126) and the Federal Water Pollution Control Act (33 U.S.C. 1321).

CASE HISTORIES

The ability of coastal states to establish oil spill liability regulations has been challenged on more than one occasion. Two cases decided by the U.S. Supreme Court are of particular relevance.

State of Maine v. Tamano

On July 22, 1972, the tanker M/V Tamano struck an outcropping off Soldiers Ledge en route to the port of Portland and discharged into the waters of Casco Bay approximately 100,000 gallons of Bunker C oil. The state of Maine brought suit to recover damages. Defendants, including owners of the Tamano, the Portland Pilots, Inc., and the United States, argued that the State could not recover costs in its *parens patriae* capacity as "owner and/or trustee for the citizens of the State." The basic argument was that the state had no independent interest in its coastal waters and their marine life to permit it to sue as *parens patriae* on behalf of its citizens.

The Supreme Court upheld the right of Maine, declaring that:

> If Maine can establish damage to her quasi-sovereign interests in her coastal waters and marine life, independent of whatever individual damages may have been sustained by her citizens, there is no apparent reason why the present action to recover such damage cannot be maintained.[11]

Askew v. American Waterways Operators

In 1970, the State of Florida established an Oil Spill Prevention and Pollution Control Act which provides for recovery of state costs in oil spill cleanup, and also imposes strict liability on shipowners and terminal facilities for oil spillage damages suffered by state or private parties. Merchant shippers, world shipping associations, members of the Florida coastal barge and towing industry, and owners and operators of oil terminal facilities or heavy industries located in Florida brought court action to enjoin application of the Florida Act (L. Fla. 1970, c 70-244). Several states, including California, Connecticut, Georgia, Hawaii, Maryland, Massachusetts, Michigan, New York, North Carolina, Texas, Virginia and Washington supported Florida.

A District Court found that the Florida law was an unconstitutional intrusion into the federal maritime domain, and that it violated provisions of the Water Quality Improvement Act of 1970 (basically now the FWPCA) and the Admiralty Extension Act as developed in *Southern Pacific Co. v. Jensen* (244 U.S. 205) and following cases (see Chapter 2).

But the United States Supreme Court reversed the District Court, declaring that:

> To rule as the District Court has done is to allow federal admiralty jurisdiction to swallow most of the police power of the States over oil spillage—an insidious form of pollution of vast concern to every coastal city or port and to all the estuaries on which the life of the ocean and the lives of the coastal people are greatly dependent.

The proposed Comprehensive Oil Pollution Liability and Compensation Act of 1977 (H.R. 2365) reflects the Supreme Court decision in *Askew v. American Waterways Operators.*   Sec. 111(a) of H.R. 2365 states:

> Except as provided in subsection (b) of this section, this title shall not be interpreted to preempt the field of liability or to preclude any State from imposing additional requirements or liability for damages, within the jurisdiction of such State, resulting from a discharge of oil.

The only preemption is to require that a federal certificate of financial responsibility, specified and required within the Act, must serve as the certificate of financial responsibility for any State liability program.

PIPELINE SAFETY

Pipeline accidents have released more oil to the marine environment than all other sources directly related to OCS operations.[12]   The largest pipeline spills have been the result of pipe rupture from anchor dragging.   One such accident in 1967 led to the release of more than 160,000 gallons of oil into the Gulf of Mexico before the rupture was discovered and corrected.

Since 1970, pipeline accidents have decreased.   The Congressional Research Service suggests that major new requirements imposed by the Bureau of Land Management are responsible for this improvement.   But their report also suggests that existent pipelines installed prior to these new requirements may in the future cause problems as they are weakened by corrosion.

An Office of Technology Assessment report summarizes the most common method of pipeline installation currently in use:

> . . . the work would be done by 175-man crews working on 300 foot 'lay barges' which can assemble and drop to the ocean floor one mile of pipeline per day.   The process involves welding 40-foot sections of steel pipe, coating them with asphalt paste or epoxy resin, bathing them in concrete to make them heavy enough to stay in place on the ocean floor, and trailing the assembled pipe over the side or stern. Smaller barges, dragging a 'jet-sled' over the ocean floor, follow the lay-barges and pump water through nozzles on the sled to dig a trench into which the pipeline settles.[12]

Current Bureau of Land Management regulations require that in water depths of 200 feet or less, all new common carrier pipelines be buried to a minimum depth of three feet. In shipping fairways and anchorage areas, pipelines must be buried at least 10 feet deep. Gathering lines between adjacent platforms do not presently require burial. Continuous line pressure monitoring systems with automatic shutoff valves or alarms, regular pipeline inspection for leaks, electrolytic protection against corrosion and special exterior coatings are also required.[1][2]

Control over pipelines is presently divided among several agencies. The authority for design standards is shared by the Office of Pipeline Safety within the Department of Transportation and the USGS within the Department of Interior.

Department of Interior authority includes all pipelines either on state submerged lands or on the Outer Continental Shelf. DOT jurisdiction is derived from:

- The Natural Gas Pipeline Safety Act of 1968, as amended (29 U.S.C. 1671 et seq.)
- The Transportation of Explosives Act (18 U.S.C. 831-835)
- Section 28 of the Mineral Leasing Act as amended (30 U.S.C. 185)
- Hazardous Materials Transportation Act (49 U.S.C. 1801 et seq.)
- Deepwater Port Act of 1974 (33 U.S.C. 1501 et seq.)

In May of 1976, DOT and Interior signed a *Memorandum of Understanding Between the Department of Transportation and The Department of the Interior Regarding Offshore Pipelines*. Under this agreement DOT and DOI will review and comment upon each other's Proposed Rule Making (NPRMS), and DOT will regulate standards for all carrier lines from the production facilities to shore.

The Department of Interior, as authorized in Section 5(c) of the Outer Continental Shelf Lands Act (67 Stat. 464) grants rights of way for pipelines in ocean (OCS) waters, and sets safety standards for gathering lines within the production field.

The Coast Guard, through its concern over oil pollution, offshore law enforcement, and navigational safety, would have

authority in certain circumstances, as would the Army Corps
of Engineers, under its navigational and dredge and fill concerns.
The Fish and Wildlife Service and the National Marine Fisheries
service operate under a mandate to consider the type of impacts
generated by pipelines, as does the Environmental Protection
Agency.

Operation of pipelines, rather than safety standards, was
supervised by the Federal Power Commission for gas, and by
the Interstate Commerce Commission for oil, as specified in
Sec 5(c) of the Outer Continental Shelf Lands Act.   These functions have since been absorbed into the Department of Energy.

MANAGEMENT INFORMATION

Obtaining timely, detailed and accurate information on OCS
and shore-related activities remains a major coastal management
problem.   It would be naive to suggest that this information
will be easily obtained, but there are several starting points that
might be useful.

OCS Lands Act Regulations (Title 30 CFR, Part 250)

OCS Lands Act Regulations (Title 30 CFR, Part 250 30 CFR
250.34) requires offshore oil and gas operators to prepare ex-
ploratory drilling plans, development plans and an application
for permit to drill, all of which provide considerable information of importance to state coastal managers.   In 1974, these
regulations were revised by Interior to require communication
of these plans and applications to affected coastal states.

OCS Order No. 12 (Gulf and Pacific Areas)

OCS Order No. 12 (Gulf and Pacific Areas) specified that,
while certain geological and geophysical information shall not
be made available to the public, in accordance with the Public
Information Act (PL 90-23), considerable information will be
available at BLM Area offices.   Such information includes:

· Form 9-152: Monthly Report of Operations
· Form 9-330: Well Completion or Recompletion Report and Log

- Form 9-331: Sundry Notices and Reports on Wells
- Form 9-331C: Application for Permit to Drill, Deepen, or Plug Back
- Form 9-1869: Quarterly Oil Well Test Report
- Form 9-1879: Semi-Annual Gas Well Test Report
- Multi-Point Back Pressure Test Report
- Sales of Lease Production

Of importance is that all accident investigation reports, pollution incident reports, facilities inspection data and records of enforcement actions are also available to the public.

BLM Area Offices

BLM maintains Atlantic, Gulf of Mexico, Pacific and Alaska Area offices, which are key contact points for coastal managers. BLM has worked with OCZM on possible state information needs and may expand its information services.

Private Industry

Oil and gas companies have long insisted upon the necessity of retaining control over much of their operational information, and this remains a point of contention that is addressed in proposed amendments to the OCS Lands Act. However, these companies would seem to have more information than anyone else. It would be of some importance for coastal water use program managers to directly contact representatives of the specific oil companies involved in OCS exploration and production. Direct contact should also be made with companies providing various processing and support services to OCS operations. If a major offshore field is involved, such contact may be a major task, but is important for good communications and information on needs, opportunities and problems.

Industrial Organizations

There are several industry-related organizations that have considerable information related to OCS activities, and many of these groups work directly with USGS on the development of standards and regulations. These groups may be able to provide information and management assistance to coastal states.   Such groups include The American Petroleum Institute, the American Society for Testing Materials, the American Society of Mechanical Engineers, the National Association of Corrosion Engineers and the American National Standards Institute.   States should view these groups not only as a potential source of information, but also as influential participants in the OCS development process, and should make every effort to keep them informed of state policies, concerns and needs.

NEW OCS MANAGEMENT SYSTEMS

CZMA Amendments

In 1976, Congress amended the Coastal Zone Management Act to include a special OCS consistency provision to Section 307.   [Sec. 307(c) (3) (B)].

Under the new provisions of Sec. 307(c) (3) (B), no federal license or permit shall be granted for OCS activities unless the proposed activity is certified to be consistent with the approved state coastal zone management program of any affected state. If a state does not concur with the proposed action, no permit or license is to be granted unless the Secretary of Commerce finds that the proposed activity is consistent with the CZMA, or necessary in the interest of national security.   To keep these provisions in perspective, however, the amendments also state, in Sec. 302, that there is a national objective of attaining a greater degree of energy self-sufficiency.   Sec. 306 is amended to include a requirement, in Sec. (c) (8), that the state program specifically consider the national interest involved in planning and siting facilities. Included are energy facilities located in, or which significantly affect, a state's coastal zone and which are necessary to meet requirements other than local in nature:

> In the case of such energy facilities, the Secretary shall find that the state has given such consideration to any applicable interstate energy plan or program.

While the states have achieved greater control over OCS activities, having been given a partial veto power over federal leases, they are also required to recognize an articulated national policy of supporting some degree of OCS development.

Section 308 of the amended CZMA establishes a Coastal Energy Impact Program (CEIP) that will allow states and local government to obtain some of the "front-end" money needed to conduct impact studies and develop necessary public services associated with energy development. Together with the Section 307 amendments, these provisions greatly increase the ability of the coastal state to be informed of and have influence over OCS decisions. Proposed modifications of the Outer Continental Shelf Lands Act may not only give coastal states even more access to the federal OCS management process, but perhaps also modify the recent CZMA amendments.

H.R. 1614 and H.R. 935

Several proposals have been made in 1977 for modification of the basic OCS leasing legislation, which is the *Outer Continental Shelf Lands Act of 1953*. At the present time several versions exist, and the final modifications, if any, cannot be predicted.

Need for State Information

Sec. 101 recognizes that states must have timely access to information regarding OCS activities and an opportunity to review and comment upon decisions relating to such activities if adverse impacts are to be anticipated and ameliorated.

Advisory Boards

Sec. 308(19) establishes Regional Outer Continental Shelf Advisory Boards. The comments and recommendations of these Boards must be considered by Interior, and the Boards are to be given access to almost all OCS data.

Of possible concern is that these Boards might somehow diminish the role of states and diminish state ability to effect comprehensive coastal planning and management systems. The actual relationship between the Boards, State CZMPs, Fishery Councils and Interior is not yet clear.

Comprehensive OCS Planning

There is a new degree of emphasis within the proposed amendments for a comprehensive OCS planning and management plan, that takes into consideration other water activities aside from oil and gas production.   Section 208(18) requires the Secretary of Interior to undertake a difficult balancing task.   The Secretary is obligated to balance between the potential for oil and gas development, potential environmental damage and potential adverse impact upon the coastal zone.

To fully achieve a literal implementation of these provisions would require a sophisticated planning and management information system and comprehensive policies on uses of the waters and submerged lands of the ocean and adjacent coastal zone that do not yet exist.

Amend CEIP Program

H.R. 935 would amend the Coastal Zone Management Act Section 308 CEIP provisions. The major change would be to earmark 25% of all federal monies obtained from OCS sales for distribution to the states under present formulae of the CEIP program.

Oil Spill Pollution Fund

Title III would provide, within the Department of Transportation, an Offshore Oil Pollution Compensation Fund of between $100 and $200 million.

CONCLUSIONS

It would appear that during 1978 major changes in the OCS management process will occur.   Current congressional action appears to be allowing a greatly expanded role for the coastal states in federal decisions, perhaps reflecting a realistic understanding of the degree to which OCS activities can affect state coastal water and land activities, and the degree to which state and local government can support or perhaps preclude certain OCS development plans.

However, it will still be left to the states to place OCS development and more generally, energy-related use of coastal waters, within a broader resource management context. The costs and benefits of necessary or desired energy development must be placed within the context of a dynamic natural system that is vulnerable, and of a growing number of activities that may be affected by or have impact upon energy-related uses of coastal waters. The 1976 amendments to the Coastal Zone Management Act place greater authority within an approved state coastal zone management program. But with that increased authority is associated an expanded responsibility to insure that necessary energy needs are met, as well as balanced against the needs for protecting the coastal water environment and accommodating a multitude of other activities.

REFERENCES

1. "Film Showed Fishing Snags Left After Oil Searches" *Fishing News International* (January 1977).
2. *Coastal Effects of Offshore Energy Systems*, Vol. II, pp. 20-108.
3. Office of Coastal Zone Management. *Threshold Paper No. 1: Boundaries*.
4. Massachusetts Office of State Planning. *Offshore Oil Development*, p. 11.
5. *Cape Codder* (May 5, 1977).
6. *Cape Codder* (March 3, 1977).
7. *Coastal Zone Management Newsletter* (February 23, 1977).
8. Congressional Research Service. *Effects of Offshore Oil and Natural Gas Development on the Coastal Zone*, p. 1.
9. *Offshore Oil Development*, p. 62.
10. Office of Coastal Zone Management. *Coastal Management Aspects of OCS Oil and Gas Development*, p. 39.
11. *Environmental Reporter*. Decisions No. 10 (June 1, 1975).
12. Congressional Research Service. *Effects of Offshore Oil and Natural Gas Development on the Coastal Zone*, p. 146.

SOURCES

1. Baldwin, P. L., and F. Malcolm. *Onshore Planning for Offshore Oil*, Conservation Foundation (1975).
2. Congressional Research Service. *Effects of Offshore Oil and Natural Gas Development on the Coastal Zone* (Library of Congress, March 1976).

3. Department of Interior. *BLM-GS Tract Selection Agreement for OCS Oil and Gas Lease Sales* (November 1976).

4. Department of Interior. *Contacts with State Governments Through the OCS Leasing Process* (January 27, 1977).

5. Department of Interior. *Inter-bureau Coordination in the Outer Continental Shelf (OCS) Minerals Program* (January 19, 1977).

6. Department of Interior. *Memorandum of Understanding Between Bureau of Land Management, Fish and Wildlife Service, and U.S. Geological Survey Concerning OCS Environmental Research and Monitoring Activities* (April 30, 1976).

7. Department of Interior. *Memorandum of Understanding Between the Department of Transportation and the Department of the Interior Regarding Offshore Pipelines* (May 6, 1976).

8. Department of Interior. *Memorandum of Understanding Between Bureau of Land Management and the Fish and Wildlife Service Concerning OCS Activities* (March 30, 1976).

9. Department of Interior. *Regulations Pertaining to Mineral Leasing, Operations and Pipelines on the Outer Continental Shelf* (August 1975).

10. Department of Interior. *Revised Outer Continental Shelf Oil and Gas Planning Schedule* (January 12, 1977).

11. Department of Urban and Regional Planning, Florida State University, and Department of Geography, University of South Florida. *Florida Coastal Policy Study: The Impact of Offshore Oil Development.* Florida Energy Office (December 1975).

12. Fish and Wildlife Service. "Oil and Gas Exploration and Development Activities in Territorial and Inland Navigable Waters and Wetlands," *Federal Register* (December 1, 1975).

13. Inman, D. L. *Preliminary Assessment of Potential Great Lakes Offshore Oil and Gas Operations*, Michigan Department of Natural Resources (November 1973).

14. Maryland Department of Natural Resources. *Maryland and Outer Continental Shelf Development: State and Local Powers to Manage Onshore Impacts of Offshore Development* (August 1976).

15. Massachusetts Office of State Planning. *Offshore Oil Development: Implications for Massachusetts Communities* (November 1976).

16. National Ocean Policy Study. *An Analysis of the Department of the Interior's Proposed Acceleration of Development of Oil and Gas on the Outer Continental Shelf*, Washington, D.C. (March 5, 1975).

17. National Ocean Policy Study. *North Sea Oil and Gas: Impact of Development on the Coastal Zone* (October 1974).

18. National Ocean Policy Study. *Outer Continental Shelf Oil and Gas Leasing Off Southern California: Analysis of Issues* (November 1974).

19. Office of Coastal Zone Management. *Coastal Management Aspects of OCS Oil and Gas Developments*, Rockville, Maryland (January 1975).

20. Office of Technology Assessment. *Coastal Effects of Offshore Energy Systems*, Volumes I, II (November 1976).

21. Studds, G., Rep. *Comprehensive Oil Pollution Liaibility and Compensation Act of 1977* (January 24, 1977).
22. Studds, G., Rep. *Tanker Safety Act of 1977.* (H.R. 3796) (February 22, 1977).
23. Hughes, J. Rep. *Outer Continental Shelf Lands Act Amendments of 1977*, (H.R. 935) (January 4, 1977).
24. Murphy, J., Rep. *Outer Continental Shelf Lands Act Amendments of 1977*, (H.R. 1614) (January 11, 1977).

PART 4

MANAGEMENT CONCEPTS

CHAPTER 11

COMPREHENSIVE COASTAL WATER MANAGEMENT

MANAGEMENT CONCEPTS

Most coastal states have been engaged for several years in some form of water resources management for fisheries, recreation, shipping or mineral extraction. But often such programs are single focus in design, and frequently are isolated from inland water planning efforts, land use planning, air quality management or deep ocean developments. As coastal water usage expands, and as the interconnection between land and water activities becomes more critical, there will be greater need to coordinate these individual programs and authorities into a comprehensive system that allows both expanded use and resource protection.

Developing a comprehensive management system for submerged lands, the water column and surface waters can seem an immense task. With the constraints of limited staff and funding, many states will as a matter of necessity implement such programs gradually, as both the need and necessary resources emerge. However, recent acceleration of OCS leasing plans, greater importation of oil, frequent tanker accidents, growing pressure upon living resources and water quality, and the continued need to facilitate increased water use suggest that the benefits of a comprehensive coastal water use management capability are already significant. The Coastal Zone Management Act and an approved state program provide a framework within which such a capability can be developed.

Objectives

The biological, geological and chemical characteristics of coastal water resources require an unusual degree of attention to the long-range objectives for their use. Since water and sediment can transmit and hold in suspension a variety of pollutants that represent limiting conditions for many possible coastal water uses, care must be taken in deciding what should be allowed and what should be regulated or prohibited. Without some comprehensive long-range goals, it is difficult to establish defensible regulations. Without specific objectives, such as maximizing commercial fishing or port expansion, it may be impossible to clearly identify which impacts are direct or significant, or even whether they are positive or negative.

Many studies and reports prepared during the past 10 years have identified the need for a national policy for coastal waters, as well as for the oceans beyond. The Coastal Zone Management Act is a direct result of the perception of this need. Through the Act, coastal states are designated as the most appropriate level of government to formulate comprehensive coastal management plans. However, the Act envisions this management effort as a partnership of public and private interests, and of cooperation between local, state and federal governments. States have neither the resources nor the authority to fully effect a comprehensive management system upon so large and important a resource as the coastal waters of the nation, without considerable local and federal assistance.

Regulation of Coastal Water Uses

The heart of the Coastal Zone Management Act lies in Section 305. Of particular importance for coastal water management are Sections 305 (b) (2), 305 (b) (3) and 305 (b) (5). These Sections require that an approved State CZMP contain:

1. "A definition of what shall constitute permissible land uses and water uses within the coastal zone which have a direct and significant impact on the coastal waters." [(Sec. 305 (b) (2)]
2. An inventory and designation of areas of particular concern. [(Sec. 305 (b) (3)]
3. Broad guidelines on priorities of uses in particular areas, including specifically those uses of lowest priority. [(Sec. 305 (b) (5)]

Definition of Coastal Water Management

Chapter 1 provided a general definition of coastal waters and of coastal water use management. At this point, a more specific definition is required.

Coastal water use management can be seen as: (a) designating what shall be permissible uses within the coastal zone, on the basis of how such uses might impact coastal waters; (b) specifically establishing a list of permissible water uses; (c) designating coastal water areas of "particular concern;" and (d) establishing priorities of use for coastal waters, including a determination of what uses shall be of lowest priority.

When stated in these terms, it becomes clear that a comprehensive coastal water use management program will be an extraordinary undertaking, and cause a dramatic shift in how coastal waters are used. For the first time, all coastal water uses would reflect deliberate public choices, determined through a state's coastal zone management program.

A comprehensive coastal water use plan would identify which activities should have greatest priority in using the submerged lands, the water column and/or the surface waters of the territorial sea. Furthermore, a comprehensive coastal water use plan would specifically identify which activities are to be permitted within coastal waters, and thus, which activities are to be prohibited. The importance of various provisions of the Coastal Zone Management Act which requires full public participation and full cooperation and participation of federal agencies, can be more fully understood in this context. No similar regulatory system presently exists on a national level, except, to some degree, for the national air traffic control system administered by the Federal Aeronautics Administration. For coastal states, it represents a tremendous responsibility, a complex management task and a major opportunity.

The National Interest

A state CZMP would specify what should and should not take place within the territorial waters of the United States. However, Congress required in the Coastal Zone Management Act that in determining priorities of use, permissible uses and areas of particular concern, full consideration be given to the national interest.

Sec. 307 (b). The Secretary shall not approve the management
program submitted by a State pursuant to Section 306 unless
the views of Federal agencies principally affected by such program have been adequately considered.

Sec. 306 (c) (1). The State (must have) developed and adopted
a management program for its coastal zone . . . after notice and
with the opportunity of full participation by relevant Federal
agencies, state agencies, local governments, regional organizations, port authorities, and other interested parties, public
and private . . . .

Since the state coastal water use program would at least in part
help more clearly determine access to the coastal waters of the state,
Congress provided that full opportunity for participation in defining
priorities and permissible uses must be extended to all interested
groups. However, it is somewhat difficult to consider the national
interest unless it has been specifically articulated. Since the Coastal
Zone Management Act in large part is designed to create a national
management system where none yet exists, it is left mainly to the
state to attempt to discover what the national interest is.

Although few specific elements are identified within the Act,
there is some guidance as to what the national interest might involve,
and how it might be determined. There exists a national interest in
defense, safe navigation, elimination of water dumping, improving
water quality, enhancing recreational and commercial fishing and
support of the American merchant fleet; but there is still no concise
statement with which states can work.

As the first state programs have reached approval stage, the difficulty of defining the national interest has emerged as a major
problem, especially in matters related to coastal waters. As described elsewhere in this book, the Department of the Navy took exception to the State of Washington program, declaring that the state
had failed to articulate the importance of defense activities in coastal
areas. The Navy felt that their interests should be identified in the
state plan as a legitimate use of coastal waters and shore areas, and
that in fact they should be identified as a priority national interest.

Another example of the difficulties arising from the national interest concept is the *American Petroleum Institute v. Robert W.
Kneccht* case. In September 1977 the American Petroleum Institute
and several other energy-related interests requested injunctive relief

in the California federal district court to keep the California Coastal Zone Management Plan from being approved by the Office of Coastal Zone Management. Their principal concern was that the California plan did not, in their opinion, give sufficient consideration of energy-related uses of coastal lands and waters as being a priority national interest.

In both instances there has emerged a concern that if some activity is not specifically designated as a priority or permissible use, it may be later declared as being "inconsistent" with the state plan. Thus increasingly, state programs will have to give detailed consideration to federal interests in coastal water use, and give specific recognition of these multiple interests in their formal state plan. This will be especially important when preparing management plans for coastal waters.

In establishing priorities of use and permissible uses for coastal waters, states must evaluate all present federal legislation to determine how it might affect coastal water use. These federal laws, unless modified by Congress, are in fact not to be changed by the coastal program, except that their administration is now significantly subject to coordination, cooperation and a consistency review. Sec.307 (e) is quite explicit about the retention of present federal law.

> Sec. 307 (e). Nothing in this title shall be construed (1) to diminish either Federal or State jurisdiction, responsibility, or rights in the field of planning, development, or control of water resources, submerged lands, or navigable waters . . . (2) as superseding, modifying, or repealing existing laws applicable to the various Federal agencies . . . .

Present federal legislation tends to be of a single-purpose nature. Much of it was established prior to the formation of comprehensive coastal management programs. As state coastal programs are implemented, it is probable that inherent inconsistencies between those programs and provisions of various federal laws will appear. If the national interest also includes wise use of coastal waters, previously enacted legislation may have to be modified to develop legislative consistency with the coastal zone management concept. It will be primarily a state task to identify necessary changes as they are encountered. It is largely through the development and implementation of state comprehensive coastal planning and management programs that the national interest in coastal waters can for the first time be articulated in a rational and detailed fashion. This is to suggest that while states are charged with working within the framework of existent law and distribution of authority, that they should also, through their unique management position, constantly evaluate present legislative frameworks and offer suggestions for possible change. It should not be accepted that present legislation and distributions of authority are the best pattern for wise coastal use, until and unless implementation of State 306 programs demonstrates this to be the case.

The Federal Water Pollution Control Act and Clean Air Act

Section 307 (f) of the CZMA stipulates that:

> Notwithstanding any other provision of this title, nothing in this title shall in any way affect any requirement (1) established by the Federal Water Control Act, as amended, or the Clean Air Act, as amended or (2) established by the Federal Government or by any state or local government pursuant to such Acts. Such requirements shall be incorporated in any program developed pursuant to this title and shall be the water pollution control and air pollution control requirements applicable to such program.

This requirement includes an implicit assumption that the standards and provisions of these two acts are consistent with wise use of coastal resources. As states gain experience through CZMA implementation, they may find that adjustments in the clean water and clean air programs would benefit coastal management objectives. Usually, states also administer the National Pollution and Discharge Elimination System (NPDES) provisions of the Federal Water Pollution Control Act, and also have the opportunity to designate air quality areas under the Clean Air Act. If these programs are closely coordinated with the coastal zone management program, significant control of the coastal water environment may be possible.

Chapter 5 described a growing number of water pollution problems that are affecting fishery resources. One of the purposes of the FWPCA, as specified in Sec. 307 (f), is to provide "for the protection and propagation of fish, shellfish, and wildlife . . . ." But present state and federal standards and programs directed at water quality management may need adjustment if they are to be consistent with coastal water management. As described in

Chapter 5, sewage treatment standards that require or encourage large amounts of chlorine may be endangering finfish or shellfish, and perhaps even human health. As quoted in that description, at least one researcher has suggested that "we don't know what we are doing." It is the opportunity and responsibility of coastal management programs to begin to make sense of the multitude of federal and state programs. While wise use of coastal waters can be a nebulous concept, it can also provide a standard against which activities and regulations can be assessed.

Tools for Coastal Water Management

There are a number of devices states can use through their coastal zone management programs to regulate the use of coastal waters. These include zoning, licensing, leasing, establishment of performance standards, control of public investments, taxation, shore access policy, permitting processes and impact statements. Each of these will be described briefly, followed by a more detailed consideration of water zoning.

Licenses and Permits

Unless preempted by federal law, states have the authority to issue permits and licenses for activities taking place in or making use of coastal waters. As part of such systems, detailed information can be required, performance standards imposed and reasonable administrative fees charged. This provides the state with a screening process as to who wants to do what. It also provides a degree of protection for coastal water users, assuring that equipment is safe, rules known and necessary technical competence obtained. However, there is the constant possibility that *interstate commerce* or areas of declared federal interest may be involved. The National Pollution Discharge and Elimination System (NPDES) of the Federal Water Pollution Control Act Amendments of 1972 is an example of a permit system that allows reasonable use while providing the public with detailed information about activities occurring within public waters and what impacts those activities may have.

Leasing

Many states are allowed by state law to lease bottom lands and in some instances, by extension, areas of the water column. The advantage of leasing over sale is that conditions can be placed in the lease to insure that if an activity begins to impart an unacceptable impact upon coastal resources, the right to use that resource can be revoked. Leasing allows use, while retaining ownership with the public. Once states have approved CZMPs in place, they may find it useful to review the language of present leasing programs, and to consider modifying them to achieve greater consistency with the CZMP.

Shore Control of Access

Most if not all coastal water activities require some type of shore access, for support facilities or initial entrance to the water environment. By regulating the pattern of *shore* use, states can also strongly influence the patterns of *water* use. Approved coastal zone management programs are supposed to have a new shore access planning element by 1978. In the preparation of these plans, consideration should be given to coastal water priorities, and to how the shore access plan can support such priorities.

Public Utilities Investments

The location and size of roads, parking lots, recreational areas, marinas, boat ramps, sewer lines and water lines can have major impact not only upon land use patterns, but also upon water use patterns. Also, public investments in harbor improvements, dredging, fish stocking or habitat improvement can influence where activities occur, what activities occur and the impact they will impart. Perhaps the easiest way to begin incorporating such investment decisions within a coastal water use program would be through comment and review upon local, state and federal projects. But in some instances a positive action program, rather than influence through reaction, may be more effective. One of the greatest difficulties in using these tools may be to gain acceptance of the need and right of coastal program participation in such decisions.

Taxation

Public tax policy is often used to encourage or discourage patterns of human activity. A tax holiday granted to a desirable project, a differential tax rate, or a special assessment to cover unusual public costs or particular private benefits are all rather familiar tools that could be extended into the management of coastal waters. The Deepwater Ports Act specifies that adjacent states can develop tax systems to recover public expenses caused by the Deepwater Port. This idea could be extended to other activities. However, there are stringent legal restrictions upon how the taxation powers can be used, and there remains a danger that desirable coastal activities may be discouraged by this or other tools, if used improperly. Also, Congress has reserved the right of taxation in some instances and it will require careful legal and fiscal analysis if such tools are to be effective.

Standards

An often effective approach is to establish standards for particular areas or activities. If standards are based upon well-founded goals and priorities, then activities can be allowed or denied use of coastal waters depending upon their ability to meet the standards. It can be difficult to monitor coastal water activities to ensure that the standards are being met. It can also be difficult to establish standards appropriate to a particular management objective. But if such standards are based upon protection of the health, safety and welfare of the residents of the state, and upon protecting the proprietary interests of the state, this may be one of the strongest tools available.

Impact Statements

Several states, such as California, Washington and Michigan, have some form of impact statement requirement. A special coastal water use impact statement could be required for critical water areas or major developments. Or present statewide impact systems could be modified to include special requirements consistent with coastal water management interests.

WATER ZONING

Water zoning is discussed further in this section in an effort to further identify and explore the complexities of implementing coastal water management.

When a state designates water Areas of Particular Concern (APC), or establishes lists of priorities and permissible or nonpermissible uses, it may in effect be establishing special water zones. Each submerged lands lease for mineral extraction or aquaculture is a form of zoning. As coastal water use grows in intensity and diversity, a systematic set of zones for the submerged lands, water column and surface waters of the coastal zone may become either a useful or necessary action.

An introductory report on this technique, entitled *Water Zoning,*[1] suggests that zones can be established either in time or space, or some combination of both. Boating can be precluded from swimming areas or dredging can be prohibited during an important shellfish spawning season. Zones could be confined to the submerged lands or the water surface. But most coastal water activities require an *activity pathway* that may include land areas, surface waters, air zones, the water column and even the submerged lands.

Existing Zones

Developing complex temporal or spatial zones for coastal waters may seem an expensive and time-consuming task, perhaps even an impossible one. But as described in Chapter 6, it is something the Navy does constantly. The Coast Guard is increasingly involved in complex surface vessel traffic control systems which involve spatial and temporal zones, and the Federal Aeronautics Administration has established major air zones on both a spatial and temporal basis. The designation of dump areas, pipeline corridors, discharge pipe locations, water quality sectors, traffic lanes, anchorage areas or marine sanctuaries are all existing examples of water zoning. In fact, one of the more important tasks for future coastal water zoning will be to properly map all of the formal and informal zones that presently exist, and evaluate them for consistency with program objectives. There are also natural zones created by tide, current, nutrient cycles, migration patterns, thermal patterns and geologic structure.

While many of these corridors, regimes, or cycles may not be visible, they constitute interconnected webs in space and time that strongly influence both human and natural activities within coastal waters.

Establishing Water Zones

Zones can be established to protect the natural water environment, to control conflicts among activities, or to protect or promote one or more preferred uses. The objective of the zone will influence the process and methodology of establishing it.

One approach that the Traverse Group continues to develop is *Space-Time Analysis.*[2] The key concept in this approach is that each activity can be described as a network of spatial and temporal parameters. The objective is to first develop activity networks for all of the uses to be considered; these are then augmented by a spatial and temporal description of the activity arena in which the uses will take place. In the case of an estuary, the description might include seasonal shifts in shellfish and finfish populations, tidal variations, bathimetry and other factors relative to the use being considered. If the spatial and temporal parameters of each activity are considered, it is expected that the maximum number of uses with the minimum amount of conflict or adverse impact upon the activity arena can be achieved.

New Hampshire may be the only state to have attempted a comprehensive coastal water zoning program. Their approach is described in Chapter 12. It is somewhat similar to Space-Time Analysis, especially in its use of inexpensive acetate overlays to do initial mapping of coastal water systems. For certain complex issues or heavily used areas, computerization of these overlays may be required, but often this additional expense is not justified. It should be emphasized that the time element in such analysis is of great importance when planning for coastal waters. Most analytical approaches developed for land use planning concentrate upon spatial parameters. But coastal water activities and coastal water natural systems are considerably more time sensitive, and temporal analysis can be critical in establishing a successful allocative pattern.

Authority to Zone

The state of Illinois is now beginning an evaluation of the possible need for one or more surface water zones within the Chicago urban area.[3] On the basis of legal analysis, they believe that they have full authority to establish such zones, if deemed necessary after further study. However, this is a complex issue and, especially in salt-water areas, state water zoning authority is not clearly established.

If a state were to create a water Area of Particular Concern and establish a list of permissible and prohibited uses for that area, it might be subject to challenge, depending upon the circumstances of the particular zoning action and which interests were affected by the regulations. It is suggested that Chapter 2 be consulted for additional discussion on this basic point, but a brief review of potential limitations will be considered here.

Coastal Zone Management Act

The CZMA gives formal federal recognition of the authority of the state to establish comprehensive management plans for the territorial waters of the United States; to establish priorities of use; designate areas of particular concern; and determine permissible and prohibited uses for these coastal waters. Furthermore, the state is given the authority to review and comment upon federal actions for the purposes of insuring, to the greatest extent possible, that such actions are consistent with the state coastal management program.

However, the act does not otherwise grant new authority to the state. Instead, existent authority is to be utilized to the fullest possible extent. It can be argued that in its requirements of what an approved program must contain, the act assumes the ability of the state to establish and enforce water zones. However, it could also be argued that such authority must exist outside of the Coastal Zone Management Act in some other articulation of state authority if the state is to have such power.

The Submerged Lands Act

As described in Chapter 2, the Submerged Lands Act, which is the basic articulation of state authority in coastal waters, resulted from a lengthy debate over control of submerged lands and hydro-carbon extraction. The act recognizes the authority of the state over the submerged lands of the territorial sea and of the living re-sources of the sea, but does not specifically mention authority to regulate the water column or surface waters.

Maritime Law

There is a complex body of national and international law that relates to ocean activities in general and to navigation in particular. Concepts of navigational servitude, right of innocent passage and other elements discussed in Chapter 2 suggest that there is a strong federal presence in any matter related to surface waters. The degree to which this body of special law precludes or constrains state coastal water management has not yet been fully or clearly articulated by Congress or the courts.

Ports and Waterways Safety Act
Rivers and Harbors Act of 1899
Proclamation 2732 of 31 May, 1947

Chapters 2 and 3 describe several federal acts or doctrines of law which may affect a state's ability to establish and enforce coastal water regulations. There appears to be a continued assumption on the part of Congress, as supported by the Constitution and several court cases, that when a regulation affects navigation or interstate commerce, federal authority will have supremacy over state law. If there is no conflict in intent or standards, state and federal law may coexist. But sometimes any state action is preempted by direct or implied congressional action. The ability of states to zone submerged lands is relatively clear. The ability of states to zone surface waters within the territorial sea is at best obscure.

The state of Washington established a tanker safety act, as de-scribed in Chapter 8, which in effect created a special water zone for large portions of Puget Sound. Within this zone, tankers larger than 125,000 DWT are prohibited. The Atlantic Richfield Com-pany (ARCO), having intended to use supertankers in this water area, has challenged this law in the courts. The company claims that the state of Washington has been preempted from establishing such regulations by the Ports and Waterways Safety Act, and that such regulations constitute an unreasonable constraint upon interstate commerce. In February of 1977, the U.S. Supreme Court agreed to hear the case. The findings of the Court could be of immense import to future efforts at coastal water zoning. But no matter what the decision is, it is likely that the ability of states to regulate surface water activities will remain at best a "grey area" of law until or unless either Congress or the courts make some definitive decision on this broad issue.

Local Government and Water Planning

The 1976 amendments to the Coastal Zone Management Act require that the state develop what amounts to an intrastate consistency review program. Local plans must be taken into account in coastal management decisions, and local government given an opportunity to comment upon major decisions prior to their implementation. This is of particular importance with reference to coastal water decisions. In many states there has been, historically, either an explicit or implicit division of authority, with local government having strong authority and responsibility down to the waterline and the state taking on more authority and responsibility as distance from shore increases. In reality, local actions almost always have some degree of impact upon adjacent waters, and many communities tend to see adjacent coastal waters as an extension of their community, whether or not they have actual authority beyond the shore. As described in Chapter 12, Oregon and Washington represent a striking exception to this pattern. But in matters such as water quality control, the state remains the primary authority even in these states.

When the state has primary authority, local governmental interests might be excluded from management decisions. The recent CZMA amendments recognize this problem and attempt to prevent it through stringent requirements for communication. However, there is also a possibility that local government will fail to notify the state of local decisions that affect coastal waters. The Coastal Zone Management Act stipulates that the state must develop some mechanism for insuring that local government does not unreasonably exclude developments of regional benefit. In a more general sense, the state is faced with the responsibility of insuring that land use planning, often conducted by local government, is supportive of and supported by water planning that is often under the authority of state and federal government.

Many states are emphasizing the role of local government in the implementation of state CZMAs. There remains a very real question as to the wisdom or likelihood of success of extending this form of administration to the submerged lands, water column and surface waters of the territorial sea. Washington State is going in that direction, although primarily for the estuarine and nearshore waters of Puget Sound. But there are several areas of possible difficulty in such an arrangement. The primary problem is one of coordination and monitoring. Especially when dealing with a deep-water activity, there are likely to be a number of federal authorities involved, and the likelihood of confusion or dispute increases with the number of government units to be dealt with. On sensitive matters of state/federal jurisdiction, the state may not wish to entrust full responsibility to local government, and it is unusual for a local community to attempt to incorporate an extensive list of national interests within its local plans and policies.

Local communities are likely to carry the burden of most impacts induced from coastal water usage. They clearly have a right and a need to participate in coastal water planning and management. Also, shore plans and policies, if carefully coordinated with water management, can support coastal water objectives. If not coordinated, effective coastal water management may not be possible. Because coastal water management is in so many ways different than coastal land management (see Chapter 1), it is possible that coastal states may wish to develop separate sets of decision rules and procedures for coastal waters and coastal lands, insofar as they pertain to the role of local government.

INCREASED MANAGEMENT: INCREASED PROBLEMS

If sustained use of coastal waters is to be assured, control over damaging impacts must be attained. Beyond this basic resource protection, which may be extremely difficult to achieve, is the need for some conflict avoidance and conflict resolution mechanism between a growing number of user groups.

However, with increased management also come a number of new problems resulting from the management effort. Obvious and important impacts of new management efforts include rising costs to the general public for government management efforts and to the coastal water user, who of necessity is often subjected to new standards and regulations.

Perhaps the most ironic and sometimes dismaying impact of new resource management programs is the identification or creation of new complex management issues that either went unnoticed or did not exist prior to the management effort. Increasingly complex trade-offs are required, along with new levels of policy analysis and detailed information.

As an example of a management-related impact, the U.S. tuna fishing industry, while having brought in record catches in 1976, faces a difficult and somewhat uncertain future as a result of marine mammal protection efforts. To protect the porpoise, the tuna industry is being subjected to increasing regulation, including technological shifts. As discussed in Chapter 5, net setting on porpoise schools has been challenged in the courts which by late 1976 resulted in a U.S. federal court order against the practice. New fish-mesh nets costing as much as $100,000 apiece seem to offer some increased protection to the porpoise, as do certain net-setting techniques. But with coastal and ocean waters subjected to increasing management scrutiny, many traditional activities will have to shift in their method or area of operation to accommodate more comprehensive multipurpose management objectives. In the past, the porpoise may have been seen primarily as a good indicator of yellowfin tuna. Now it is seen as a valuable marine species that must be accommodated and protected, along with the yellowfin fishery. Especially when dealing with natural marine species or systems, there is often little leeway, and it is the human activity that must be adjusted.

As reported in the April, 1977, issue of *National Fisherman*, South Carolina trawler fishermen are currently cooperating in a study on the impact of trawling upon loggerhead turtles, which in time may be officially considered an endangered species. The fishermen hope to demonstrate that shrimp trawlers do not capture a significant number of loggerhead turtles incidental to their fishing operations, and that present trawling techniques do not have any significant impact upon loggerhead turtle mortality rates. The South Carolina fishermen correctly perceive that if the loggerhead becomes a managed marine species, there may be some pressure to modify the equipment or practices of the $25 million southeastern shrimp fishery, unless the trawling can be shown to be of little impact upon loggerhead survival.

Increased Costs

An area that requires much more information and policy evaluation at both the state and federal levels is the question of direct and secondary costs of a particular management system. This refers not so much to the direct operating costs of staffing a program and enforcing its policies, although these too are critical considerations. Rather, reference is made to the need for yellowfin tuna fishermen to change net types and test new net-setting techniques, at increased cost, to accommodate a new policy for porpoise. A perhaps more dramatic example can be found in Lake Michigan, where Michigan regulations have led to the virtual collapse of the commercial fishing industry. While seining equipment and methods may eventually allow the redevelopment of a commercial fishery that in the past relied upon gill nets, it will represent a major cost to many individuals.

While these may be necessary costs for the sustained use of finite resources by a growing number of user groups, these costs are significant and at some point should be directly evaluated as part of the resource allocation process.

Prior Claims

As an associated consideration, it is often the case in coastal water management that to accommodate some new activity, a traditional user will have to be either displaced or required to alter usage patterns. It cannot be over emphasized that what can occur and how it can occur within coastal waters depends in large part upon how many activities and people and what level of vitality and durability of natural environment are desired. At one level, such a statement is overly obvious. But for most coastal water use management programs, the implications are major. If porpoise survival is of little or no concern, then the yellowfin tuna harvesting techniques that can or do destroy large numbers of porpoise may be the most economical and efficient methods, and could be allowed to continue. But when porpoise are to be protected, or water quality is to be kept within some specified range or the continued use of coastal areas for certain industry is to be assured, then certain performance standards or types, ranges, and locations of behavior must be imposed upon other potentially competing activities, including new ones and also those which already exist and may be heavily resistent to change.

Choosing Alternatives

Coastal water use management is in large part a question of making choices among and between alternative patterns of natural systems and human activities, allocating air, water and submerged land space and resources to some limited number of interest groups. Some of the allocative decisions are outside of human control at this time, with natural dynamics still being the primary definition of what can and cannot occur.

Other allocative decisions are made by Congress or the Office of the President, in decisions to encourage ocean development, establish certain air quality standards, or protect a given marine species. But the state, through its CZMP, will increasingly be faced with both the responsibility and the opportunity of making coastal water use allocative choices. Each state, each resource manager, will bring expertise and regional needs to the choices, but certain general concepts or rules may be of value:

1. The greater the changes which a use will impart upon coastal waters, the fewer the other uses that can take place within that same activity arena. There may be several important exceptions to this concept, but it is often a useful starting point.

2. Water or coastal dependency is both a very solid and a very soft concept for allocation. Some activities could not take place without a coastal or water location. That does not in itself enshrine such "dependent" uses with a superior claim to finite and valuable resources. Some activities could take place outside the coastal zone, but at increased cost. Thus there is more than one type of dependency; it could be based upon costs of operation, costs of moving from present site, or some actual technical coastal-dependent requirement.

3. Most, if not all, human activities could benefit in some way from a coastal location, if only as a matter of aesthetics, *e.g.*, a major apartment complex or corporate headquarters. Thus, there may be few purely technical rules or concepts by which these difficult allocative choices can be made.

Consistency

The degree to which states are able to review and comment upon federal actions and to enforce consistency with the approved coastal management plan may determine the success of the state program. The state has been given primary authority for coastal water management. But several important authorities are reserved for the federal government. It has been suggested in Chapter 2 that the Coastal Zone Management Act may be unrealistic in its continuance of the present distribution of authority, with neither federal or state government having sufficient authority to really achieve comprehensive coastal management (land and water). The Coastal Zone Management Act relies to an extraordinary degree upon cooperation and the consistency provisions of Section 307. It is presently impossible to accurately discuss how or if the consistency provisions of the act will work, since final rules and regulations are still in the formative stages and already a point of contention. But unless the final rules and regulations are quite different than currently anticipated, they could serve as a positive and essential tool for coastal water management.

The submerged lands, water column and surface waters of the coastal zone repersent an immense management task in terms of sheer size. The biological, chemical and geological complexity of this resource, combined with historical and emerging patterns of human use make it a task beyond the resources of most, if not all, states at the present time. Yet there is a need for planning and management. This can be achieved if the resources of the many federal agencies involved in ocean and coastal planning and management can be used. Consistency is usually envisioned as relating to some project, such as a proposed deepwater port. However, it is possible that consistency could also apply to federal actions such as the design and implementation of a research program. If the state were able to secure agreement with a federal agency before it commenced an inventory or research project, it might assure that the resulting information was of use not only to the federal agency, but also to the state coastal management program.

Strategies for enforcement and monitoring could be developed among states, and between states and federal agencies such as the Coast Guard. It is arguable that even the budget formulation process of one or more federal agencies could have a direct and significant impact upon a state's coastal waters. While comment and review upon federal activities will always be a politically sensitive matter, it has the potential to bring more resources to a coastal management program than would otherwise be available. Federal agencies have thousands of people, access to major data banks, extensive research reports, expensive equipment and a legal mandate for action which, if linked to the state coastal program, could enable a comprehensive approach that states by themselves would not be able to achieve. Because of a strong concern about possible conflicts between federal and state interests, the consistency provisions of the act have often been seen in a negative contentious role. Yet these provisions could also be used creatively in a positive cooperative effort to link federal and state actions.

Long-Range Planning

A review of present state coastal management efforts reveals that in most instances the coastal water element is much less comprehensive than the land use element. Also, coastal water management seems in many cases to be devoted almost entirely to a reactive mode, developing procedures for reacting to proposed actions by non-CZMP interests. Having a reactive capability is certainly a necessary part of a coastal water management program and it is perhaps the best place to start. But reacting, if not accompanied by comprehensive planning, is in fact management by default. Under such conditions, wise use can be neither defined nor assured.

The nation has an extraordinary opportunity to develop comprehensive coastal water use plans and management systems now, at a point when coastal water use appears ready to greatly accelerate. There is an opportunity, but also a need, to determine just what wise use might be and how to promote it. It is a question of what should, rather than what does, occur.

The 1976 amendments to the Coastal Zone Management
Act require the establishment of comprehensive shore access
plans by 1978. Many states, as part of their access planning,
have adopted the allocative principle of coastal dependency.
Those activities that are most dependent upon a coastal location are given priority over activities that could be located
elsewhere. While dependency is often a relative term rather
than a concrete measurable standard, it seems to provide most
states with a workable rule for resolving conflicts between competing activities.

However, one long-range consequence of this policy is to
maximize future pressure upon coastal waters. Also, it leaves
undecided, which coastal-dependent activities should be given
priority. Some activities are dependent upon shorelands, some
upon estuaries, some upon the deep waters of the territorial
sea. The concept of dependency as it is being articulated today
may provide some guidance in sorting out competing land uses.
But when and if comprehensive coastal water planning is undertaken, this principle may require some refinement. Perhaps
coastal land access should reflect priorities of use established
for coastal waters.

Conclusions

Coastal waters receive impacts from the ocean, from the atmosphere and from the land. Concurrently, coastal water management decisions can have direct and significant impacts upon
these other systems. Attempting to establish some structured
priority of uses for this complex, sensitive and valuable system
represents a new level of resource management. However, the
need for such management is great. The ability of coastal waters to support abundant populations of finfish and shellfish
may be at stake. Certainly, major problems exist. And maximum benefit cannot result unless there is some order, some
evaluation, some monitoring and some regulation. Coastal water management need not impair economic activity. In fact,
it is a necessary adjunct to increased use. The Coastal Zone
Management Act provides the states with sufficient authority
to undertake comprehensive management programs for coastal
waters. However, because of the present distribution of

authority between federal and state interests, full development and successful implementation of comprehensive coastal water management cannot occur without the cooperation and participation of both interests. It is possible, even probable, that this present mixture of authority will have to be adjusted. And as national interests shifts to areas such as comprehensive energy planning and management, a unified coastal water management program may temporarily be more difficult to achieve, rather than facilitated. Yet there is sufficent authority and congressional mandate within the Coastal Zone Management Act to allow an initial attempt at comprehensive coastal water management by coastal states. And there are also a growing number of reasons why it should be undertaken.

REFERENCES

1. Ryner, P. C. *Water Zoning: The Management of Surface Activity on Lakes, Streams, Rivers and Bays*, University of Michigan Sea Grant Program (March 1973).
2. Ryner, P. C. *Environmental Impact Planning*, The Traverse Group, Ann Arbor.
3. Schaefer, C., Illinois Coastal Zone Management Program. Personal communication (April 1977).

CHAPTER 12

STATE MANAGEMENT PROFILES

ILLINOIS

The Great Lakes contains 95,000 square miles of water, or some 65 trillion gallons, which represents almost one fifth of the world's freshwater supply. The lakes and their connecting waterways form the world's largest inland water transportation route, which is 2,300 miles long.

Within this system, Lake Michigan is the only lake that is entirely within United States jurisdiction. Control over its waters and submerged lands is shared by Wisconsin, Illinois, Indiana and Michigan. This lake is 300 miles long, in places is more than 900 feet deep and has 1600 miles of shoreline.

Illinois, with only 60 miles of shoreline, has one of the shortest coastal zones of any coastal state. However, it faces a number of complex issues, and is the site of extensive shoreline development, including the city of Chicago and the Calumet river port complex. While Illinois is still in the development stages of its coastal zone management program, it has already established some coastal water use approaches that are of interest. Three elements of particular interest are its fisheries management program, its management approach to offshore sand deposits, and growing interest in surface water zoning.

Fisheries

Lake Michigan's Fisheries were greatly reduced during the 1950s and 1960s by lamprey predation and overfishing. A measurable deterioration of water quality further accelerated the decline. Illinois, as part of its coastal zone management program, has identified commercial and recreational fisheries as priority uses of lake waters, and during the 1977 work program planned to initiate a research project to rebuild the previous indigenous fisheries, especially lake trout.

Extensive plantings of lake trout have occurred; however, the system is basically an artificial one as the lake trout are not reproducing naturally. While it is not clear why there is reproduction failure, the Illinois Coastal Zone Program, in cooperation with the state's Department of Conservation (DOC) will conduct a stocking program. An attempt will be made to reestablish natural breeding areas within a series of submerged dolomite reefs that once functioned in that capacity.

Of particular interest is that after having established the priority of fisheries management, the Illinois program further established that the offshore reefs constituted a critical habitat resource and designated them as Geographic Areas of Particular Concern (GAPCs) as provided for in the Coastal Zone Management Act. Illinois felt that a **GAPC** designation would afford these reefs a greater degree of protection and would also insure a degree of management attention that might not otherwise exist. Other states, such as Massachusetts, feel that **GAPC** designations for such areas are not necessary.

One critical problem that Illinois shares with other Great Lakes states is a serious water contamination by PCBs. As described in Chapter 5, this is an increasing problem that appears to be extending into many coastal waters. In some instances, such as occurs in Michigan, it has been determined that the bioaccumulation of PCBs within some fish, particularly coho salmon, is so severe as to render the fish a human health hazard. The impact this water quality problem will have upon Illinois' fisheries management program is unclear at this time. It could be involved in the reproduction failures of lake trout and might render various finfish unfit for human consumption.

Air Quality and Water Quality

Potentially important to coastal water management efforts in other states is the finding that atmospheric transport and deposition of air pollutants may be a significant mechanism for water pollution. In a program report, the Illinois Coastal Zone Agency states that:

> A special study demonstrated that atmospheric fallout of PCBs may be contributing much greater amounts of PCBs to Lake Michigan than are being contributed by industrial and municipal effluent.

In future years, regulation of atmospheric emissions may be a critical part of coastal water use management.

Sand Deposits

Sand deposits beneath coastal waters represent an important resource, one that is of growing commercial interest in many coastal states. Illinois has taken a somewhat unique approach to this resource that may be of interest to other coastal states.

First, Illinois, with the cooperation of the State Geologic Survey, has developed full maps of all sand deposits within nearshore areas. Based upon hydrographic studies and a series of drilling profiles, these maps provide a clear inventory of all significant nearshore sand deposits at a scale of 1 inch = 200 feet.

Having established this inventory, the state considered declaring these deposits a GAPC. However, it was decided that the state already had full authority over the deposits and that GAPC designation would not have any particular advantage. The policy which the state has established is that these deposits will not be used for commercial purposes. Instead, they will be used only for beach nourishment.

Much of the Illinois shore is highly erodible and shore erosion can be critical, especially during years of high lake levels. Also, unlike some other coastal states, Illinois has a very limited supply of coastal sand. Thus the official priority use of this resource is for beach nourishment.

During the 1977-78 work program the state intends to initiate a first test program of beach enrichment. Sand will be dredged from offshore deposits, transported by barge four miles north, and deposited on the Illinois Beach State Park, which is a GAPC in the northern sector of the state's coastal zone. Placed at the shore's edge, it is expected that nearshore currents will distribute the sand in a natural pattern of deposition. After careful monitoring and any necessary adjustment, this program will be extended down the shore.

Dredge Spoil Disposal

The United States Environmental Protection Agency has prohibited any further disposal of dredge spoil within the coastal waters of the State. At present, polluted dredge spoil is deposited in a specially designated diked area in the Calumet harbor region (although there is a need for further provisions). As for clean spoil, the Corps of Engineers has agreed to the deposition of this material as *strategic stockpiles* along the shore, as part of the artificial beach enrichment program.

Surface Water Zoning

Because of its intensive development, the Illinois coastal zone generates and attracts a considerable amount of surface water activity. Initially other coastal management issues and tasks were identified as being of greater priority, but during the next year Illinois intends to give detailed consideration to the possible need, benefits and methods of establishing a surface water zoning system, such as discussed in Chapter 11.

Of primary attention will be the possible conflicts among various types of boating activities, and between these and other surface water uses, such as swimming. As discussed in Chapter 11, this might include either temporal or spatial zoning, or some combination of the two. Illinois has determined that it has full authority to implement such techniques, if they become necessary.

Military Use of Coastal Waters

There is one surface water conflict that may be difficult to resolve. North of Chicago, the Navy operates the Great Lakes

Naval Training Center, which, as federal land, is excluded from the Illinois coastal zone management program. However, as part of its use of this shore property, the Navy has established a rifle range that is oriented so that rifle bullets travel over the surface of the coastal waters. Considering that high-powered military rifles are used, this is judged to be a hazard.

To prevent accidents, the Navy has marked the range on charts, and during times of use, the water area is marked by flags and buoys. In effect, this has become a military water zone, a water extension of the Naval base.

However, it is not clear to the state that the Navy has the authority to establish such a zone. Illinois claims full authority; furthermore, the state has established a set of permissible uses, as required in the Coastal Zone Management Act of 1972 for approved programs. It has established two general categories of use: high- and low-priority uses. The principal criterion for inclusion in a high-priority category is dependence upon a coastal location: the activity must, of necessity, have to be located on or near the water. Other uses that do not have to be located within the coastal zone are assigned to the low-priority category.

With reference to the Great Lakes Naval Training Center, the state feels that the use of surface waters for a rifle range is not only a hazardous use, but an unnecessary one.

> Apart from the harbor facilities for naval operations, none of the activities on such bases are truly coastal dependent. Further military uses in the coastal zone which are not coastal-dependent are not considered desirable or necessary.

The Department of the Navy appears to see national defense and national security not only as important matters of national interest, but also as highest or overriding priority uses for coastal areas. In this instance, they have indicated that the training center is seen as an essential part of its national defense and national security responsibilities.

The issue is an important one, for while the concept of surface or subsurface zoning may be rather straightforward, the ability to implement and enforce such zones will depend upon cooperation and acceptance of the legitimacy of such zones by coastal users. As in many other coastal areas, the Navy has established a de facto surface water zone for the use of military weapons.

The state has declared such a use as being neither necessary nor desirable. Since the range is located near recreational boating facilities, it is probable that the state would consider establishing a surface water recreational zone that would tend to preclude the use of water areas for rifle range purposes. The shore facility is excluded from the coastal program, but it is not clear that the adjoining coastal waters are. Without specific congressional mandate, it is questionable that the Navy has authority to establish such a water use zone, at least without state concurrence. When the activity is not coastal-dependent, as appears to be the case in this instance, then the Navy's possible claim to overriding national interest is perhaps even weaker.

However, this reflects a serious national coastal water issue. Nationwide, there are extensive water areas that lie within state coastal waters yet have been designated as military zones. If necessary, national defense considerations are to be met, and if an endless set of conflicts is to be avoided, it will probably be necessary to take a broad examination of this situation and reevaluate the purpose, location and necessity of each such military zone. As nonmilitary uses of coastal water resources increase, so might the conflicts between state and DOD interests. (Chapter 6 discusses this in more detail.)

Offshore Islands

An interesting coastal water use issue exists in terms of planned construction of large offshore islands in Lake Michigan, along the Chicago urban coastline. These islands would be built with fill material from subway and storm sewer construction.

The use of coastal waters and submerged lands will have a major effect on the coastal zone. Current studies are underway to determine the positive and negative impacts of such a development. How this development would fit into a comprehensive water use zoning program has not yet been established. The Illinois Coastal Zone Management Office is working with the City of Chicago in examining this proposed development. Water zoning techniques have been proposed for control of water uses, once the islands are completed.

FLORIDA

Florida has one of the largest coastal zones in the United States, and due to its location within the Gulf of Mexico and Atlantic Ocean systems, it is particularly rich in natural marine systems. Some 25 million tourists visit the state each year, and its coastal zone is one of the primary reasons for this industry. The coastal waters, including a water zone of three nautical miles in the Atlantic Ocean and three leagues, or nine nautical miles, in the Gulf of Mexico, encompasses some 10,000 square miles, almost one fifth the size of the state's upland areas. It incorporates vital transportation networks, defense and research activities, open waters, mangrove islands, oyster bars, coral reefs, grass flats and coastal marshes. It is a sensitive system that has experienced problems with "red tides," growing indications of finfish problems, and incredible rates of residential and commercial growth. It is also, however, a state with a number of resource management programs that if successfully combined, would constitute a strong coastal water management program.

Coastal Coordinating Council

In 1970 the State Legislature passed Act 259, which created a Coastal Coordinating Council that functioned until 1975, when a state reorganization took place. It passed on many of the functions and responsibilities of the Council to the Bureau of Coastal Zone Planning, which currently directs the Florida CZMP effort. Of several mandates placed upon the Council, perhaps the most important was to:

> develop a comprehensive state plan for the protection, development and zoning of the coastal zone, making maximum use of any federal funding for this purpose.

While that comprehensive plan was never completed, a considerable amount of important work was done, and serves as the basis for the present Florida coastal management effort. This work included a detailed inventory of the Florida coast, the development of most of the presently used Florida coastal management concepts, and the preparation of a series of maps of use for local planning.

Local Government

Florida's CZMP places considerable reliance upon local units
of government, although not as much as Oregon or Washington.
The Local Government Comprehensive Planning Act of 1975
requires local government units to develop comprehensive plans
by 1979. The strategy of the Bureau of Coastal Zone Planning
is to provide local government units with detailed inventory
information and a set of state policies and guidelines, for incorporation within the local program. At this time a nine-volume
Florida Regional Coastal Zone Management Atlas is being dis-
tributed to local governments as a detailed planning and management assistance effort. Reflecting earlier efforts of the Council,
this Atlas uses graphic presentations in an effective manner.

Permissible Uses

The waters and lands of the coastal zone have been classified
into one of three categories: protection, conservation or development. These categories reflect state CZMP objectives and
policies, and articulate what uses should occur in each area.
It is expected that these classifications will be incorporated into
the local comprehensive plans and also be acknowledged by
other state agencies.

State Waters

Reflecting the state water quality management program, the
waters of the state have been divided into five classes. These
waters, as well as a set of coastal land types, were further divided
into one of three principal management categories mentioned
above. The Bureau has developed matrices for each of the three
categories which should be consulted for complete details (see
citation at end of presentation). These matrices include all the
land and water types that fit within the use category, and then
list factors such as priority use, state's management objectives,
general state policy, responsible state agencies and existing state
regulations. Thus, in the preservation category, Class II waters
have as a priority use, shellfish harvesting and propagation of
marine life. As a general state policy, no dredging will be

allowed in Class II waters except for the maintenance of existent navigation channels. In the *conservation* category, spoil islands have as a use priority recreation, bird/wildlife habitat and aesthetics. The general state policy is to keep spoil islands as undeveloped areas to be utilized as green areas, bird habitat and water-oriented recreation areas.

This is a water zoning system, combined with a coastal land zoning system, and it is intended to be used by both state and local government. To simplify and clarify, maps showing these areas are printed with red for preservation, yellow for conservation and green for development. This can then serve as one basis for consistency review, and for communication with federal agencies regarding state policies and concerns.

Aquatic Sanctuaries

Florida has placed considerable emphasis upon land and near-shore planning and management, as have the majority of coastal states at this time. In addition, Florida also has developed a somewhat unusual water management system involving the designation of certain submerged land areas as Aquatic Sanctuaries.

The concept of aquatic preserves was first formulated in 1968. Aquatic Sanctuaries are to have one or a combination of three management purposes: biological, aesthetic or scientific. The marine sanctuaries concepts and provisions of Title III of the Marine Protection, Research and Sanctuaries Act of 1972 are in part based upon this system, and are similar in nature.

These sanctuaries are not preserves, but special management zones in which specific uses will be given priority and other uses allowed to the degree that they do not violate that priority. While further rules and regulations can be adopted in the future, existing regulations are quite minimal in that many activities are allowed. The only activities specifically excluded are oil and gas drilling and dredging for the primary purpose of obtaining fill for upland development.

There are now 31 aquatic preserves. They have been established not by Bureau policy, but by the legislature through passage of the Florida Aquatic Preserve Act of 1975. These have been further incorporated within the state management program by designating 30 of the sanctuaries as proposed APCs, as described in the Coastal Zone Management Act.

MASSACHUSETTS

Massachusetts has an extensive coastline of 12,000 miles, and has a considerable history of coastal water use. Boston harbor serves as a major urban port. There is significant commercial fishing and fish processing and extensive recreation, including activities associated with the Cape Cod National Seashore. The coastal management program staff includes 23 professionals and is in the process of developing a complex program.

The Massachusetts program has developed objectives and policies for six major categories of concern:

1) Marine Environment
2) Coastal Hazards
3) Visual Environment
4) Ports and Harbors
5) Recreation
6) Energy

Also, the program has identified three levels of critical areas:

1) Significant Resource Areas
2) Areas for Preservation and Restoration (APR)
3) Special Assistance Areas

These critical area designations are conceptually related to a calculation of capability and suitability. Thus an area considered unique for their contribution to marine productivity might be designated as an APR. Within the APR, a set of performance standards and prohibited uses would be established, to protect specified values.

To implement this and other elements of the State CZMP, Massachusetts has relied heavily upon a networking system of administration. This is especially important for Massachusetts, where water management legislation has been in force for several years. As compared with some other coastal states, Massachusetts already has many "in-place" systems.

The network of administrative linkages necessary to implement marine water policies includes CZMP interfaces with at least the following specific programs:

- Coastal Wetlands Restriction Program
- Wetlands Program
- Waterways Program
- Ocean Sanctuaries
- Division of Marine Fisheries
- Division of Marine and Recreational Vehicles
- Hazardous Waste Program
- Energy Facilities Siting Council
- Department of Public Works
- Division of Water Pollution Control
- Water Resources Commission
- Division of Mineral Resources

This list does not include federal agencies or programs, which would also be involved. While Massachusetts is not unique in this situation, it is a good example of a state in which previously a number of single- or narrow-focus programs had been established. The task is to combine the expertise and sometimes conflicting interests of these programs into a comprehensive and cohesive whole.

The Massachusetts network is complex, involving several levels of review (see Massachusetts Coastal Zone Management Preview, Chapter 3). The basic coastal zone management program will be housed within the State Executive Office of Environmental Affairs (EOEA), and the basic state coastal zone management legislation is an amendment to the state law affecting EOEA. Maps, identification of significant coastal areas and of policies for these areas, and review of state and federal environmental impact statements will provide a flow of information which EOEA will monitor. Another key aspect of the Massachusetts networking system will be to place CZMP staff within the regional offices of the Department of Environmental Quality Engineering (DEQE). These CZMP staff will help integrate new coastal management policy into existing programs and permit systems and will issue certificates of consistency as appropriate. Again, the emphasis is upon coordinating and influencing "on-line" programs rather than attempting an entirely new major level of planning and management. Massachusetts is indeed unusual in the number and type of existent coastal resource management programs it has. One of the more interesting of these, in terms of coastal water management, is its Ocean Sanctuaries program.

Ocean Sanctuaries

Massachusetts has established, under state law, four ocean sanctuaries, independent of the more recent coastal management efforts, and these sanctuaries will now serve as a major component in the state's coastal water element of the CZMP.

When taken as a whole, these sanctuaries cover a majority of the state's territorial waters, leaving in effect only two principal corridors for commercial activities. It is in reality a form of water zoning. However, each sanctuary has been established separately, with specific objectives and restrictions, and the method in which they are actually incorporated into future water use allocations within the state coastal management program is not yet fully clear.

Perhaps the principal advantage of having these declared legislated sanctuaries is that it provides the state with an extra degree of legitimacy in reviewing the actions of a proposed coastal water activity, including those sponsored by one or more federal agencies. As described in Chapter 11, there is presently some concern that if a state has not articulated a specific set of interests, that state's ability to review and comment upon a federal project under the consistency provisions may be limited. These sanctuaries not only establish a set of permissible and nonpermissible uses, but also a special management framework within which virtually any activity would be subject to state review.

An Example: Cape Cod Ocean Sanctuary

To provide a buffer zone within the coastal waters adjacent to the Cape Cod National Seashore, Massachusetts adopted the Cape Cod Ocean Sanctuary Act in 1970 (Ch. 132A, Sec. 13-16). This buffer area, described by metes and bounds, is established with a specific management objective and a set of permissible and nonpermissible uses. The purpose is to insure that:

"The Cape Cod Ocean Sanctuary . . . shall be protected from any exploitation, development or activity that would seriously alter or otherwise endanger the ecology or the appearance of the ocean, the seabed, or subsoil thereof, or the adjacent Cape Cod National Seashore."

The sanctuary serves as a buffer to the seashore through its control of coastal water uses. Since the principal purposes of the seashore are to preserve the natural shore system and accommodate public recreation, the adjacent coastal waters are reserved, under the sanctuaries act, to compatible activities. With State approval, permissible uses include:

- laying of cables
- channel and shore protection projects
- navigational aids or improvements with federal and state approval
- harvesting of fish and shellfish
- temporary educational and scientific study facilities
- seabed aquaculture structures

Prohibited activities include:

- building of any structure on the seabed or under subsoil
- removal of sand, gravel, other minerals, gases, or oils, with the exception of sand and gravel extracted for the purpose of shore protection and beach restoration, provided that such projects are limited to the adjacent public beaches
- dredge and spoil activities
- dumping of commercial or industrial waste
- commercial advertising

In 1971, a sanctuary was established for Cape Cod Bay, and also a Cape and Islands Ocean Sanctuary, including the waters and submerged lands of Nantucket Sound and Buzzard Bay. The Cape and Islands Sanctuary, reflecting the political process by which these management zones were established, includes an allowance of industrial thermal discharge under state permit control, but otherwise is similar to the first two sanctuaries.

In 1972, a fourth sanctuary was established for the coastal waters from Cape Ann north to the New Hampshire border, completing the current system and bringing the majority of state waters under special management consideration. Combined with the Significant Resource Areas (SRA) and Areas for Preservation or Restoration (APR), this provides a considerable degree of specific state-level management objectives for the coastal waters of Massachusetts. The ocean sanctuaries preceded the national Coastal Zone Management Act and provided a coastal water management framework which is now being incorporated into a stronger than usual water element in the CZMP.

NEW HAMPSHIRE[1]

New Hampshire is one of the smaller coastal states and has a coastal zone management program staff of only four people. This helps explain a program emphasis upon networking among existing state agencies and programs, and upon the use of existing information. Of particular interest is the suitability/capability analysis that has been done for New Hampshire's coastal waters and the states method of identifying permissible coastal water uses.

Background

New Hampshire enjoys the somewhat unusual position of having total control over its submerged lands. While most if not all states exercise control over water use, there are few states that have not given a partial use right to private interests through permit, license or lease. Yet in New Hampshire, leases for commercial shellfishing, aquaculture or offshore mining have never been granted. This may considerably ease the problem of dealing with prior claims when future allocative decisions are made. Lobster fishing licenses are the only exception to this pattern.

Natural Limitations

As with many parts of the eastern coast, New Hampshire waters are relatively shallow. This represents a natural impediment to some of the projected future uses of coastal waters. Only shallow draft vessels can be accommodated without major dredging or the construction of a deepwater port (an idea that has been suggested). Thus some of the new LNG tankers, with a draft of 80 feet or more, will not be able to use New Hampshire waters. For the same reason, many of the major OCS-related impacts of a possible Georges Bank discovery would not occur in such shallow waters. However, pipelines, gas processing facilities, deepwater ports and other future demands upon the state's coastal waters are very real possibilities, and the state CZMP has proceeded as if OCS and similar developments will impact the state at some future point. For example, a land and water impact study is expected to be completed in June which will then lead to an identification of land and water areas that could support possible OCS-related activities or facilities.

Capability/Suitability Analysis for Coastal Waters

The New Hampshire CZMP contracted with the Strafford Rockingham Regional Council to undertake a *Coastal Zone Water Use Capability Analysis,*[2] which has led to the designation on official state maps of use classifications for all state coastal waters.

The preliminary inventory was based upon existing data, and New Hampshire CZMP personnel stress the amount of information that can be obtained from existing sources, if enough creative searching is done. One of the most useful recent sources has been the federal Environmental Impact Statement (EIS) prepared for the controversial Seabrook nuclear power plant. As the Capability report observes:

> The development of a rational methodology for water use
> capability classification, properly based on detailed scientific
> and economic data, would require *years of effort* and *hundreds
> of thousands of dollars.*[3] (Emphasis added)

The initial inventory survey included:

1. Coastal ecosystems
2. Marine and estuarine species
3. Bottom sediments—offshore
4. Existing marine uses
5. Potential marine uses

Several maps were then prepared, to develop an overlay system similar to that often used in land-use planning. The maps included:

1. Spawning areas—major marine species
2. Offshore fishery areas of importance to New Hampshire
3. Clamming and oystering areas (three maps)

    4. Offshore fisheries—Portsmouth and Gloucester landings [1]
    5. Existing areas—offshore
    6. Offshore sand and gravel deposits

The inventory and analysis process led to a determination that the following uses are likely to significantly increase in New Hampshire coastal waters:

    1. Commercial fishing/lobstering
    2. Recreational fishing/boating/swimming/visual enjoyment
    3. Ocean shipping/anchorage
    4. National defense
    5. Research and education
    6. Cable routes

Possible increased water uses include:

    1. Deepwater ports
    2. Offshore sand and gravel mining
    3. Aquaculture
    4. Ocean dumping

Having developed this initial inventory on a map overlay system, several concepts of capability/suitability analysis were considered. Eventually, a seven-parameter system was chosen, with emphasis upon existing uses and natural systems as a measure against future suitability. The seven parameters include:

    1. Location and intensity of existing coastal and estuarine water uses.
    2. Presence or proximity of marine and estuarine habitats of significant value to the natural environment.
    3. Existing land uses adjacent to these water areas and their suitability for development.
    4. Presence of marine and estuarine resources of potential value to man, either indirectly, commercially, or recreationally.
    5. Expected impact on coastal waters and adjacent land of possible future coastal and estuarine uses either in, or in close proximity

---

[1]New Hampshire has limited fish processing facilities, so a significant portion of the commercial catch is off-loaded in Massachusetts, making it difficult to determine total catch from state waters.

to, waters under New Hampshire control. This includes increased
intensity of present use as well as introduction of new uses.

6. Presence of physical restrictions on development and use (shallow
water depths, bridges, currents).

7. Water quality.

By applying these seven factors to the inventory maps, a four-
category classification system for estuarine, coastal and some ocean
waters was developed. Planning maps were printed with these areas
designated. Similar to the approach of Florida, this leads to a good-
to-bad continuum of use capability. The categories include:

Area I (excellent): capable of supporting nearly all water uses
that may be technologically feasible.

Area II (good): capable of supporting nearly all water uses
that may be technologically feasible, but un-
suited to ocean dumping, sand and gravel mining,
and deepwater ports.

Area III (fair): capable of supporting small boat anchorages,
commercial fishing and lobstering, underwater
cables, aquaculture, recreational fishing and
boating, pipelines in conjunction with a deepwater port, research and education, swimming
and aesthetic enjoyment.

Area IV (poor): capable of supporting aquaculture, commercial fishing and lobstering, recreational
fishing and boating, research and education,
swimming and aesthetic enjoyment.

When applied to the coastal waters of New Hampshire, there are
no Area I classifications within the three-mile territorial sea, the
nearest area being 14 miles from shore, at a point when potential
oil spills or other adverse impacts from major intensive uses are biologically, chemically, physically and aesthetically isolated from
critical nearshore areas. A two-mile water buffer zone is established
under Area III designation. Proximity to shore and to adjacent areas
of high recreational value prevents a higher classification.

Capability Area II classifications exist beyond this buffer zone,
in which ocean shipping, recreational and commercial fishing, and
more intensive uses can take place. "Distance from adjacent land
and the less critical nature of natural systems in this area reduces the
chance of significant adverse impact from heavier uses."[4]

It is interesting that this system formalizes what several states have intuitively established on a more general basis. This formal system may provide a much greater degree of acceptance by potential users, as well as by the courts, although it is still somewhat "soft" and may well require considerable augmentation if the probable and possible use increases do occur. Future Environmental Impact Statements may be one source of information for such improvement.

This approach is similar to a water or ice-surface zoning system suggested by Ryner,[5] but the New Hampshire program has not established zones, but general areas of capability instead. From these general areas, concepts of permissible uses and priorities of use have been derived, and are contained in proposed state legislation.[6] Thus, the actual impact of this capability analysis must be evaluated within the context of the proposed land and water use management system.

Similar to the approach of several other coastal states, New Hampshire has classified its coastal management zone into three parts: primary, secondary and tertiary zones. The primary zone is the focus of the water-use management program, and includes:

1. all tidal estuarine and oceanic waters to the seaward limits of New Hampshire jurisdiction;
2. all submerged lands under such waters;
3. all intertidal zones;
4. all tidal and freshwater wetlands, bodies of salt- and directly adjacent freshwater, and beaches and sand dunes adjacent to tidal waters;
5. all islands surrounded by tidal waters; and
6. all lands extending inland from the mean high water mark, or from the landward edge of the tidal wetland where present, to either the first 20-foot elevation contour which is noncyclical within the state of New Hampshire, or a horizontal distance of 1000 feet, whichever is farthest.

Within this primary zone, rather than directing management efforts at resource characteristics or activities, New Hampshire has chosen to focus on direct and significant impacts. It is these impacts that would bring an activity under consistency review of the state program, and for which rules and regulations will be promulgated. These impacts, or characteristics of water activities, include:

1. Degrade water quality through the introduction into coastal waters of sediments, nutrients, toxic heavy metals, petroleum hydrocarbons, oxygen-demanding chemicals, or pathogenic bacteria.
2. Deplete ground or surface water supplies.
3. Result in saltwater intrusion into ground water supplies.
4. Impede ground water recharge.
5. Degrade land or water wildlife, or essential wildlife habitat or fish or shellfish concentration areas.
6. Alter the composition, migration patterns, distribution, or other population characteristic of the natural species.
7. Overexploit or despoil living or nonliving marine resources.
8. Erode beaches, sand dunes, rocky shores, or other areas of the shoreline.
9. Encroach upon or displace tidal wetlands, beaches, sand dunes, or rocky shores.
10. Result in erosion into or sedimentation in coastal waters.
11. Impede navigation.
12. Impede the ebb and flood of tidal waters.
13. Degrade air quality.
14. Result in aesthetic degradation.
15. Preempt or impede a higher priority use.

This list of possible impacts indicates the areas of state concern within the coastal zone. More specific concerns are identified in APC designations. Within a year of the passage of the Act, specific APC designations are to be made and placed on official state maps. The proposed legislation contains the APC categories, along with specified highest and lowest priority uses. Water APCs include:

1. tidal wetlands
2. fish spawning or concentration areas
3. shellfish (including lobster) concentration areas
4. areas of scenic importance
5. areas of cultural and historical significance
6. areas where development is dependent upon utilization of, or access to coastal waters
7. offshore sand and gravel deposits
8. other unusual natural areas

Due to historical factors of coastal resource characteristics, private economic decisions and public policy, New Hampshire does not yet have major problems of coastal water use. However, their approach to coastal water use management is presently one of the most advanced of any of the coastal states.

Implementation of the concepts, formulation of specific rules and regulations, court tests and actual user conflicts will provide a clearer indication of this management system than is now possible. By placing emphasis upon present patterns of use, potential impacts and inherent fragilities, there is a base, a spine, upon which further regulations or programs can be developed. It seems a promising approach.

WASHINGTON[1-8]

The state of Washington contains a very complex coastal water system that includes Pacific Ocean waters and also the waters of Puget Sound. In terms of sheer size, this represents a major task for planning and management. There are also major fishing, recreational and commercial shipping activities, as well as a significant concentration of naval activities and facilities. Thus Washington, with the first approved Sec. 306 coastal zone management program, is faced with major issues of multiple use and multiple jurisdiction.

Considering this somewhat imposing management task, it is all the more surprising to note the degree to which coastal water uses are to be planned and managed by local rather than state government. As with a few other states, such as Oregon and Florida, Washington had an active program of comprehensive coastal planning in place before federal CZM funds became available.

Shorelands Management Act of 1971

Under this Act, a Department of Ecology (DOE), which now administers the State CZMP, was to develop guidelines for land and water uses within the state's coastal zone. Based upon those guidelines, local units of government (counties and cities) were to establish comprehensive management plans. These are continuing to be developed and implemented under the now expanded state coastal management program. Under the Act, which has become the principal element in the State CZMP, any substantial development must receive a local permit to occur. "Substantial" is defined, with some exemptions, as involving a market value of more than $1000 or as any action that would materially interfere with normal public use of the water or shorelines of the state.

The Department of Ecology cannot approve or deny local permit decisions, but it does have a specified period of time in which to appeal the decision to an independent hearings board created by the State Shorelands Management Act, called the Shorelines Hearings Board. DOE and other state agencies have used this process, and it can be used to challenge either a permit approval or denial. Local units of government can also use the Board as a means of challenging state regulations or guidelines.

Because local government plays so strong a role in water use allocation decisions in Washington, it is essential that they be given sufficient tools and technical assistance to carry out this task. Towards that objective, DOE has devoted a considerable amount of its first year 306 funding to the development of a *County Planning Manual.* This is directed primarily to the waters of Puget Sound.

Planning Manual

The Manual is intended to answer three basic questions:

1. Who has ownership and/or jurisdiction over a particular site? What regulatory programs affect the area? What are the legal issues and policies affecting the decision?
2. What is the natural system or habitat that exists at and around the site? How should the site be managed?
3. Should the proposed use be allowed to locate on the site? If so, under what conditions?

A Legal Analysis section will attempt to clarify the extent of local authority over a given use and/or site and identify potential conflicts of authority. A Habitat section describes Puget Sound systems, including flora and fauna, associated physical and geological conditions, and an approximate indication of tolerance levels. A simplified key, based on substrate type, is included for easy identification by local planners. A Uses and Performance Standards section develops an impact matrix suggestive of the work of Sorenson, the impact approach contained in Volume 5 of the *National Estuary Study,* and to a limited extent, the space-time approach discussed in Chapter 11.

If successful, this manual should not only serve as an impact planning guide, but also as a directory of the goals, objectives, rules and procedures of the state's coastal program. The emphasis of this work is upon Puget Sound waters and Pacific Ocean coastal waters are, for the most part, left out of this planning and management effort. Given the priorities of the state and the patterns of coastal water use development, it may be a reasonable emphasis at this time, but the methodology of the manual might require considerable modification for deepwater allocative decisions.

State Department of Natural Resources

Some of the bottom lands of the state are in private ownership. When the state Constitution was formed in 1889, the State asserted ownership of the beds and shores of all navigable waters in the state up to and including the line of ordinary high tide. But prior to August 8, 1971, the state was authorized to sell tidelands and shorelands to private individuals, companies and corporations, which it did. Chapter 217, established in 1971 and amended in 1974, prohibited any further sales, except to public agencies. However, as in most states, *leasing* is still permitted.

The State Department of Natural Resources (DNR) owns approximately 11 square miles of harbor area, 140 square miles of shorelands, 205 square miles of tidelands, 1250 square miles of beds of navigable lakes and rivers and 1800 square miles of beds of navigable tidal waters. The Washington Parks and Recreation commission also has some holdings, but DNR is the major administrator of marine lands. In the early 1970s, DNR embarked upon a program of planning for these marine lands. The marine lands were divided into seven management areas, and then a three-phase planning and management program was implemented. At this point several principles and concepts have been adopted.

One of the principles of use allocation is to avoid the permanent use of a site by a single activity when that site can support multiple use. In fact, multiple use is the principal allocative concept which DNR is required, by law, to use.

DNR Policy

At this time, DNR has six basic allocation policies that it applies to its marine lands. They deal with navigation and commerce; public use; food, mineral and chemical production; protection of the natural marine environment; use by abutting upland owners; and revenue production.

Navigation. Shallow draft uses, such as barge terminals and marinas, will be preferred over deep draft uses in areas requiring extensive maintenance dredging.

Provisions will be made to minimize interference with surface navigation even though other uses have been allocated.

Public Use. Whenever practical, leases of first-class tidelands will provide for public access to the water.

In recognition of the increasing impact of the recreating public on the state's beaches, new programs will be devoted to public education about stewardship of state marine resources.

Food, Mineral and Chemical Production. Tidelands and beds of navigable waters especially valuable for aquaculture will be so designated and protected from conflicting uses that would limit their utility for this purpose.

Provisions will be made to insure that traditional commercial fishing areas are protected from competing uses that create obstructions.

Whenever structures are used for aquaculture on the beds of navigable waters, they shall be located to minimize the interference with navigation and fishing and adverse visual impacts.

Protection of the Natural Marine Environment. Easements or leases for the development of underwater piplines and cables will not be granted except where adverse environmental impacts can be shown to be less than the impact of upland alternative(s), and when granted will include proper provisions to insure against substantial or irrevocable damage to the environment.

Structures and uses on marine lands will be designed to provide for safe passage of migrating animals whose life cycle is dependent on such migration.

Uses by Abutting Upland Owners. When tidelands are leased to someone other than the abutting upland owner, such leases will provide for the abutting owner to reach the beds of navigable waters.

To reduce the burden on marinas, private mooring buoys and floats associated with shoreline residences will be encouraged.

Revenue Production. When the effects of marine uses have an identifiable adverse impact on Department of Natural Resources land, a value will be placed on the loss or impact and charged to the user.

Available revenue from leasing of marine lands shall be used for marine land management programs that are of direct benefit to the public.

There are many more provisions under each policy heading, but this sample indicates the type and specificity of policy that has been established. It is worth noting that under Uses by Abutting Upland Owners private mooring buoys and floats are encouraged. In some states there has been increased effort to consolidate such facilities so as to minimize surface obstructions.

In future there will be a need for very close coordination between DNR leasing policy and DOE administration of the state coastal zone management program, which relies so heavily upon local decisions. The administrative network is asked to accomplish much, to insure that local decisions and DNR decisions mesh into a consistent state water use planning and management effort.

OREGON[1]

In several states, the basic concepts of a comprehensive coastal zone management program had already been developed by the time that Sec. 305 program development grants became available through the federal Coastal Zone Management Act. Oregon, and to a similar extent, Washington, exemplify coastal states where advanced comprehensive land and water use planning was well underway by the mid-1970s. These existing programs provide a strong basis for coastal management, and also to a great extent determine what form the state's CZMP will take. In Oregon, the coastal management program is based upon the Oregon Land Use Act (ORS 197). This legislation, often referred to as Senate Bill 100, places considerable emphasis upon the role of local government.

Similar to the planning history of Florida, Oregon established an Oregon Coastal Conservation and Development Commission (OCCDC) from 1971-1975. This Commission developed an initial inventory of coastal resources, hazards and needs; developed coastal land and water resource policies; and developed methods of implementing a comprehensive coastal management program.

Land Use Act[2]

The Land Use Act (SB 100) requires that a Land Conservation and Development Commission (LCDC) develop and adopt goals and guidelines which would become the state policy for management of land, air and water resources. Also, the Act requires that each city and county develop comprehensive plans in conformance with the goals. State agencies and special districts must, through their plans and actions, also conform both to the goals and to local comprehensive plans. Thus, the key to Oregon's coastal zone management program is the goals developed by the state. On December 18, 1976, LCDC adopted four new goals, for a total of 19. Two of these new goals are of particular interest with reference to coastal water use management.

Goal 16: Estuarine Resources

By June 15, 1977, LCDC was to complete a classification of Oregon estuaries and specify the most intensive level of development or alteration that can occur within each estuary. As part of its comprehensive planning, each city and county will develop estuary management plans that will reflect the Oregon Estuary Classification and the provisions of the goal, which includes the requirement that:

> estuary plans and activities shall protect the estuarine ecosystem, including its natural biological productivity, habitat, diversity, unique features and water quality. Dredge, fill or other reduction or degradation of these natural values by man shall be allowed only: (a) if required for navigation or other water-dependent uses that require an estuarine location; (b) if public need is demonstrated; (c) if no alternative upland locations exist; and (d) if adverse impacts are minimized as much as feasible.

All estuaries are to be classified as natural, conservation or development. All estuaries must have natural areas, and unless designated in the Oregon Estuary Classification for preservation, all estuaries must also have conservation areas. Each estuary will have its own priorities, but the goal identifies as general priorities, from highest to lowest:

1. uses that maintain the integrity of the estuarine ecosystem;
2. water-dependent uses requiring estuarine location, as consistent with the overall Oregon Estuarine Classification;
3. water-related uses that do not degrade or reduce the natural estuarine resources and values; and
4. nondependent, nonrelated uses that do not alter, reduce, or degrade the estuarine resources and values.

In effect, this estuarine goal establishes a system of estuarine use plans, which may include surface water zones that specify types of use. This is treated as a natural extension of the local government land planning, out into the waters of the state. Since the same unit of government, under state supervision and review, establishes plans for both the coastal lands and adjacent coastal waters, the two elements can be readily coordinated. Consequently, land uses adjacent to designated natural estuarine areas will not involve industrial activities, and presumably coastal lands adjacent to designated development estuarine areas would not be reserved for wilderness or low-intensity recreation. As a further part of the estuarine goal, an impact assessment is required, either at the time of plan formulation, or, for activities not considered in the estuarine plan, prior to activity approval.

The local estuarine plans will not be conceptually isolated from the rest of the coastal managment program, and will reflect the other 18 goals. For example, it appears that Oregon will attempt to concentrate major new commercial port development at one of three existent large ports. The other, smaller ports would be classified as such, and the local plans would be monitored to insure that for these ports major new development was not contemplated.

Goal 19: Ocean Resources[3]

Within the Oregon Program, as with virtually all other state CZMPs at this time, much less emphasis is placed upon deepwater planning and management than upon estuarine and nearshore areas. In Oregon, aside from some important commercial fishing activities, there is relatively little offshore activity, and thus pragmatic considerations of program priority have placed most attention upon the more crowded and pressing nearshore problems. The Ocean Resources goal is much less detailed than the other 18, and it is possible that until more problems emerge, that it may remain a somewhat low-priority aspect of the program.

Priorities of Use. Goal 19 specifies that:

> Since *renewable* ocean resources and uses, such as food production, water quality, navigation, recreation, and aesthetic enjoyment, will provide greater long-term benefits than will *non-renewable* resources, such plans and activities shall give *clear priority to the proper management and protection of renewable resources.* (emphasis added)

The State policy of favoring renewable resources, such as finfish, over nonrenewable resources, such as oil or gas, has not escaped the notice of federal agencies, and there has been some expression of concern that such a policy might hamper OCS developments.[4]

At this point, the state is not formulating a specific management plan for its ocean resources. It is instead a reactive permit process. Given the state's emphasis upon local planning, it is difficult to see how local governments could develop an adequate plan in an area where they are not traditionally involved. At this time there is a strong feeling that a comprehensive plan, similar to that being established for Oregon's estuaries, is in fact not necessary.

Permit Requirements

Although Oregon has determined that a comprehensive plan is not required for its territorial waters, beyond those being prepared for estuarine systems, it still has one of the most comprehensive permit systems. The Ocean Resources Guidelines suggest that permits for development on the Oregon continental shelf should:

1. designate areas within the proposed development where activities such as exploration and extraction will be prohibited;
2. specify methods and equipment to be used and standards to be met;

3. *require the developer to finance monitoring and inspection of the development by the appropriate state agency;*
4. require the developer to be liable for individual or public damage caused by the development and to post adequate bonding or other evidence of financial responsibility to cover damages;
5. specify the extent of restoration that must be accomplished where appropriate, when the development is finished;
6. specify that the state or federal government may revoke or modify a permit to prevent or halt damage to the environment and that such revocation or modification will recognize vested rights of the developer;
7. require the developer to describe the extent and magnitude of onshore support and operation facilities and their social, economic and environmental impacts on the Oregon coast; and
8. be available for public review and comment before issuance.

There are certain potential problems with this set of permit requirements. Obviously they are oriented towards OCS oil and gas development and seem adequate for such activities. However, the guidelines apply to any activity occurring on, in or beneath the continental shelf within state waters, not just oil and gas extraction. It is not clear that all the provisions developed by Oregon are appropriate for every coastal water activity. For example, is it necessary or appropriate for commercial fishermen to pay for monitoring and inspection? Perhaps it is, but the economic yield of various activities differs widely, and such a requirement might preclude an activity in some instances, especially in those where no or little economic yield is involved. Some degree of resolution might be achieved through a careful program definition of "development" or by formulating sets of permit requirements for various types of offshore acitvities.

REFERENCES

Massachusetts

1. Kraczkiewicz, M., Massachusetts coastal program coordinator. Personal communication (May 5, 1977).

New Hampshire

1. Goss, L. and staff of New Hampshire coastal zone management program, Concord, New Hampshire. Personal communication (May 6, 1977).
2. Strafford Rockingham Regional Council. *Coastal Zone Water Use Capability Analysis* (September 1976).
3. *Ibid.*, p. 1.
4. *Coastal Zone Water Use Capability Analysis*, p. 12.
5. Ryner, Peter. *Water Zoning: The Management of Surface Activity on Lakes, Streams, Rivers and Bays.* University of Michigan, Sea Grant Program (March 1973).
6. "Coastal Resources Management Program." SB 189.

Oregon

1. Based upon interview with Ted LaRoe, Salem, Oregon, on May 13, 1977, and upon Oregon CZMP materials cited below.
2. Oregon Land Conservation and Development Commission. *Oregon Coastal Management Program* (1976).
3. Land Conservation and Development Commisssion. *Statewide Planning Goals and Guidelines 16, 17, 18, & 19 for Coastal Resources Effective 1 January 1977* (December 1976).
4. See citation No. 1.

SOURCES

Illinois

Illinois Division of Water Resources. *Illinois Coastal Zone Management Program: Preliminary Draft* (November 1976).

Schaefer, C., Illinois Program Coordinator. Personal communication. Chicago (April 1977).

Taussig, Wexler and Shaw, Ltd. *The Legal Framework: Toward A Management Program*, Illinois Department of Transportation (June 1976).

U.S. Army Corps of Engineers. *Chicago Harbor, Chicago River and Calumet Harbor and River Confined Dredge Disposal Area Site Selection Study*, Chicago District (November 1976).

Florida

Bureau of Coastal Zone Planning. *Florida Coastal Zone Management Program (Section 305) Status Report to the Governor and Cabinet* (January 1977).
Bureau of Coastal Zone Planning. *Proposed Geographic Areas of Particular Concern* (January 1977).
Bureau of Coastal Zone Planning. *Suggested State Objectives, Policy and Criteria for Coastal Management in Florida* (January 1977).
Center for Governmental Responsibility. *Analysis of Laws Relating to Florida Coastal Zone Management* (October 1976).
Coastal Coordinating Council. *An Oceanographic Survey of the Florida Territorial Sea of Escambia and Santa Rosa Counties* (November 1973).
Florida Aquatic Preserve Act of 1975.
Florida Inter-Agency Advisory Committee on Submerged Land Management. *A Proposed System of Aquatic Preserves* (November 12, 1968).
Local Government Comprehensive Planning Act of 1975.
Myers, J. C.,and R. C. Glassen. *Guidelines for Management of Florida's Aquatic Preserves,* Florida State University (March 1977).
Staff of Bureau of Coastal Zone Planning in Tallahassee. Personal communication (April 1977).

Massachusetts

Executive Office of Environmental Affairs. *Boston Harbor* (April 1977).
Executive Office of Environmental Affairs. *Massachusetts Coastal Zone Management Preview*, State of Massachusetts (November 1976).

New Hampshire

Strafford Rockingham Regional Council. *Inventory and Designation of Geographic Areas of Particular Concern* (April 1977).
Strafford Rockingham Regional Council. *Land and Water Use Capability* (Map) (September 1975).
Strafford Rockingham Regional Council. *Land/Water Use and Vegetative Cover* (Map) (September 1975).

Washington

Boule, M. Corff and Shapior, Inc. Personal communication (May 12, 1977).
Corff and Shapior, Inc. *Coastal Aquatic Area Management Study*, Seattle (April 1977).
Farley, P. J. *Maps of Aquatic Habitats for Areas of Puget Sound*, Shoreline Community College, Seattle.
Office of Coastal Zone Management. *State of Washington Coastal Zone Management Program Final Environmental Impact Statement*, Washington, D.C. (April 9, 1976).

Peterson, D. Washington Department of Ecology. Personal communication (May 12, 1977).

State of Washington Department of Natural Resources. *A Circular of General Information Relating to State Owned Aquatic Lands*, Olympia (1974).

State of Washington Department of Natural Resources. *The Land Use Allocation Plan, Department of Natural Resources Managed Marine Lands* (February 14, 1973).

Vining, R. Washington Department of Natural Resources. Personal communication (May 11, 1977).

INDEX

INDEX